Religion
in the 18th Century

Publications of
the McMaster University
Association for 18th-Century Studies

Copies of all volumes are available from Garland Publishing, Inc.

Religion
in the 18th Century

edited by
R.E. Morton
J.D. Browning

Garland Publishing, Inc.
New York & London
1979

The Association for 18th-Century Studies

McMaster University
Hamilton, Ontario
Canada

Library of Congress Cataloging in Publication Data

Main entry under title:
Religion in the 18th century.

(Publications of the McMaster University Association for 18th-Century Studies ; v. 6)
  1. Europe—Religion—18th century—Addresses, essays, lectures.   2. United States—Religion—To 1800—Addresses, essays, lectures.   I. Morton, Richard Everett, 1930–
II. Browning, John Dudley, 1942–   III. Series: McMaster University Association for 18th-Century Studies. Publications ; v. 6.
BL690.R44   209'.033   79-17715
ISBN 0-8240-4005-8

Printed on acid-free, 250-year-life paper
Manufactured in the United States of America

CONTENTS

INTRODUCTION

The contributors to this volume study the diverse and pervasive influence of religious beliefs and institutions in eighteenth-century Europe and colonial America. They also record the decline of that influence on the intellectual, moral and social life of the time. The book opens with Randolph Currie's inquiry into the elder Bach's religious faith as professed through an esoteric scheme of musical cryptography. It closes with Michael A. Meyer's sad chronicle of the religious alienation of European Jews uneasily settled in England. Bach spent his musical gifts in celebrating truths consecrated by the church in which he remained spiritually at home. Belonging to an age that was passing away, he remained undisturbed in his faith by new currents of thought that were eroding the old creeds all around him. It is not Bach, the Christian composer, but the expatriate merchant Jew, with his allegiance divided between market-place and synagogue, who represents the eighteenth-century experience of being pressed into a secular society. Each of the intervening essays treats an aspect of the changes in moral view and social life that came about in the eighteenth century as religious conviction and authority faltered under the weight of philosophical criticism and heavy new economic burdens.

In the opening pages of his classic study of eighteenth-century English thought, Sir Leslie Stephen speaks of the general law of persistence which tends to the preservation of religious doctrine. A system of belief providing men with a settled order of ideas for the interpretation of the meaning and value of their personal lives is resistant to change. It is further stabilized by its capacity to uphold the moral views and practices of the age and to vindicate prevailing social and political institutions. But these very grounds of religion's endurance are vulnerable to changes occurring within other dimensions of culture. Ideas about the nature of things change as men adjust their vision of reality to new speculations and discoveries. Moral question long thought to have been definitively answered, are re-opened as certain matters of right come to be seen as matters of privilege, certain duties as barren of social utility, certain prohibitions as gratuitously repressive. Forms of social life and political organization are transformed in the process of adapting to changing economic conditions. As the theoretical opinions and practical policies which religious beliefs had supported at the beginning of the eighteenth century evolved, religion itself fell victim to the general law of displacement.

The full significance of great intellectual and social movements shows itself only in retrospect. Men living in the midst of events are at a disadvantage in that the contemporary scene which they try to understand belongs to a play of events that is unfinished. Since the historian is aware of the outcome of these events, he can discern the meaning and direction of earlier stages. Another advantage of historical hindsight is the view it gives of seemingly independent trains of events moving toward a common destination. Lacking a prophetic vision of the secular society of the future, the eighteenth-century Jansenist could not see that his liberal programme of politicl reform was tending in the same direction as the *philosophe's* investigations of the psychopathology of religious belief. However, the utilitarian ethic advocated by spokesmen for the "Second" Jansenism shows itself in Cyril O'Keefe's study "The Jansenists and the Englightenment in France" as attuned to the humanist philosophy of the period. The doctrine "that the ultimate duty of the governor is to look to the happiness of his people" better accommodates the secular spirit of the Enlightenment than the asceticism which had originally inspired the founder of the Order.

Frank E. Manuel appropriately borrows the overture to his study of "The Philosophes and the Psychology of Everyday Religion" from Hume's *Natural History of Religion.* "The classical eighteenth-century document in the psychology of religion," as Manuel calls Hume's work, contributed equally to the author's celebrity in France and to his infamy at home. In a letter sent from Paris in 1764 Hume wrote: "I believe, taking the Continent of Europe, from Petersburg to Lisbon, and from Bergen to Naples, there is not one that ever heard my Name who has not heard of it with advantage, both in point of Morals & Genius. I do not believe there is one Englishman in fifty, who, if he heard that I had broke my Neck to night, would not be rejoic'd with it." Hume thought that he understood why he was without honour in his own country. Responding to a request for his impressions of France, he asks: "Shall I begin with the Points, in which it most differs from England, viz., the general Regard pay'd to Genius and Learning;...or the almost universal Contempt of all Religion, among both Sexes, and among all Ranks of Men?" In England, thinkers and writers were treated with indifference, and, if they were not affluent, with contempt. "Hence that Nation are relapsing fast into the deepest Stupidity, Christianity & Ignorance."

Hume had already settled in his own mind the question of the truth of religion, both revealed and natural, before visiting the salons of the enlightened. Judged by the usual canons of historical evidence, he concluded in his *Enquiry Concerning Human Understanding:* "no human testimony can have such a force as to prove a miracle, and make it a just foundation for any such system of religion." So much for theism; and he allows little more to deism: "one simple, tho' somewhat ambiguous, at least undefin'd Proposition, *that the Cause or Causes of Order in the Universe probably bear some remote analogy to human Intelligence,*" constitutes the whole of the defensible content of natural theology. On the presumption that almost all religious teaching was likely false, Hume explored, as did the *philosophes*, the sub-rational grounds of religious belief, and there are striking parallels between his own speculations and those of his French confrères.

On the fundamental point, however, Hume and the more radical *philosophes* were unreconciled, and this difference in their positions was a source of disappointment on both sides. Hume's scepticism enjoined suspension of judgement on questions to which neither reason nor experience could provide answers. Dogmatic theism and dogmatic atheism seemed to him equally arrogant and irresponsible in violating a region of the unknowable, and he was dismayed by the self-assurance with which such militants as Holbach pronounced on topics that so far outdistanced the capacities of the human mind. Hume's scrupulousness was taken by the savants of the rue Royale as a vestige of bigotry that had unaccountably survived the evolution of his generally enlightened philosophy. In this connexion a story has come down in several versions, of which the following is Diderot's as recalled by Ernest Campbell Mossner in his life of Hume:

> The first time that M. Hume found himself at the table of the Baron, he was seated beside him. I don't know for what purpose the English philosopher took it into his head to remark to the Baron that he did not believe in atheists, that he had never seen any. The Baron said to him: "Count how many we are here." "We are eighteen." The Baron added: "It isn't too bad a showing to be able to point out to you fifteen at once: the three others haven't made up their minds."

Hume did agree with the *philosophes* about religion's pernicious moral influence. In his earlier works Hume had contended merely for the independence of morality from religious sanctions, which claim was required by his project for a naturalistic ethics developed as part of a general, empirical science of human nature. Morality could be understood as safely based upon human need and desire and the principles of social organization required to satisfy them. Having once viewed religious belief and institutions as ethically irrelevant, Hume came to see them as positively harmful.

According to Hume's theory of the shaping of the religious consciousness, the individual is coerced by an external authority invested with punitive powers into professing hypocritically to believe what offends his common sense. Through the habit of dissimulation thus engendered, irrational beliefs are internalized, and the victim feels conscience bound to believe, through an act of will, what he does not really believe in his heart. His anxious inner conflict is resolved by hardening himself in self-deception and revenging himself upon any dissident who threatens to revive his deeply repressed doubts. Such is the psychological mechanism which accounts for the bigotry and fanaticism whose evil effects on society are frequently documented in *The History of England,* where Hume makes the following characteristic observation of the Puritan Commonwealth: "It must, however, be confessed, that the wretched fanaticism which so much infected the parliamentary party was no less destructive of taste and science, than all law and order. Gaiety and wit were proscribed; human learning despised; freedom of inquiry detested; cant and hypocrisy alone encouraged."

Thus Hume wrote about the psychology and politics of religion in an idiom which the *philosophes* found congenial and which encouraged them to expect that Christianity would be extinct by the end of the eighteenth century. This result, they thought, would mark a notable stage in moral progress. In a universe more coherent than our own the three cardinal values, Truth, Beauty, and Virtue, would be so related that the artistic and moral improvement of mankind would keep pace with the advancement of knowledge. The eighteenth-century agnostic or atheist who derived his beliefs about the world and human prospects from natural science and secular history was closer to the truth, I daresay, from the Roman Catholic misssionary who expected an eternal reward for his devoted service to others. Even so, one cannot contemplate the lives recalled by W.J. Eccles in "The Role of the Church in New France" without realizing that men and women may be inspired by false beliefs to lives of noble dedication. There were edifying pages in the annals of the Church that Hume and the *philosophes* overlooked, as they also overlooked those precious works of art whose conception outside of the derided system of religious belief is unimaginable.

The predicted elevation of the moral quality of social life did not invariably attend the decline of the Church's position, as we learn from William J. Callahan's "A Social Contract: the Poor, the Privileged and the Church in Eighteenth-Century Spain." One result of the liberal attack upon ecclesiastical privilege and revenue was that the charitable work formerly done by the Spanish Church and its various orders had to be taken over by the State. Although a pot-luck factor operated within both administrations, the spiritually motivated one seems to have been the more effective of the two in alleviating the distress of poverty. But the morally interesting difference between religiously motivated charity and bureaucratically administered welfare is apparent in the two views they take of the recipient of alms: as a fellow man whose misery one is enjoined by God to relieve; as a social problem with which an efficient government is expected to deal. Admittedly, the theological theory of charity should appear intolerable, both intellectually and morally, to an enlightened man: "The intention of God in making some men rich is to make them charitable; those chosen to enjoy this grace do so because they have been made instruments of divine mercy": a proposition as well calculated to justify an inequitable, hierarchical society as to solicit donations. Nor were contributors who planned to collect dividends in perpetuity in an after-life moved by purely altruistic motives and reasonable expectations. Still, there was an element of humanity and tolerance in the face-to-face encounter of the eighteenth-century Spanish bishop or nobleman with the pauper that would have no place in the secular, welfare state with its poorhouses — "virtual prisons," as Callahan tells us.

In "The Sanctification of Nature" Grant Sampson follows a theme which appears somewhat poignant in retrospect. The considerable intellectual and literary abilities spent on the works which Sampson treats were deployed in an enterprise bound to fail. Physico-theology set itself the single-minded task of reconciling natural science and religion by accommodating a scientific cosmology conceived upon mathematical and mechanistic principles within a system of belief derived from myth, legend and metaphysical speculation. Its elaborate constructions were eloquent and edifying, but based upon foundations that were logically flawed.

Eighteenth-century English writers on natural religion were chiefly inspired by the *Philosophiae Naturalis Principia Mathematica*, in which Newton's demonstration of the mathematical simplicity and coherence of the laws governing the physical universe provided compelling evidence of Design from which to infer the existence of a first Cause, "very well skilled in mechanicks and geometry," Newton judged. "This most beautiful system of the sun, planets, and comets," he wrote in the General Scholium of the second edition of the *Principia*, "could only proceed from the counsel and dominion of an intelligent and powerful Being." Scientific explanation in terms of mechanical causation left much unexplained, and Newton encouraged speculative extrapolations of scientific results to religious questions which eluded direct investigation by the experimental method. It was Hume who showed that the Argument from Design proceeded by violating the methodological principles of the science upon which Newtonian theologians claimed to model natural religion. The "religious hypothesis," he concluded, was "uncertain and useless," extending far beyond the realm of empirically verifiable assertion.

If truth is served by discarding needless assumptions and untestable hypotheses — by "removing some of the rubbish that lies in the way of knowledge," as Locke said of his own work — then Hume's efforts to de-sanctify nature were rightly directed. It may be that quite independently of Hume's critique of the Design Argument, natural religion became a depleted literary resource, exhausted by the eighteenth-century English writers whose voluminous work Sampson reviews.

Within late eighteenth-century popular religion, which Gerald R. Cragg discusses in "Wesley and the Renewal of English Religion," evidences of divinity in nature would still be adduced in sermons addressed to the "ordinary intellect," to use Stephen's elitist expression. By the turn of the century, when William Paley's *Natural Theology* (1802) appeared, the "higher intellect" (also Stephen's term) was already alienated from natural religion. A mechanistic conception of nature — by most intellectuals presupposed, rather than maintained as an explicit creed — displaced the reverential doctrine of the physico-theologians.

The secular view of nature cohered with the theories of mathematical physics and fitted the facts more tidily than did the spiritual one. From the point of view of science, wherein truth is the over-riding value, the de-sanctification of nature marked an intellectual advance. With respect to certain other, non-cognitive values, however, an irredeemable loss was incurred when the idea of nature as a divine creation was displaced by the concept of a self-contained machine. It is of the essence of a machine to serve human ends and purposes; lacking intrinsic value, its function is to be useful. So nature came to be regarded, and so it has been used, with fateful consequences which even (perhaps especially) the most enlightened thinkers of the eighteenth century could not foresee.

Learning how the world looked to men and women of former times, like travel in foreign lands, lets us see our own time and place in broader and truer perspective. The historian defines our present situation by retracing the course of events which led up to it. Of the many lines of historical force which converged from the eighteenth century upon the twentieth, religion is a particularly instructive one to explore, as the reader of the following studies will discover.

James Noxon
McMaster University

Bach's Faith:
An Interpretation Based on
the Evidence of the Organ Works

Bach's religion would hardly be of interest today if it were not for his supremely great music. Probably the best reason for even discussing the subject is the possibility that such an investigation might somehow expand our comprehension of the composer's incredibly rich art. In the process, we might also gain insight into the nature of the religious experience as it affected one of the most profound figures of the early eighteenth century.

I must admit I had strong reservations about writing on the subject of Bach's religion. Perhaps this is the sort of topic which should be approached at the end of a lifetime of study and reflection — if at all. It may, in fact, be presumptuous even to attempt to discuss another man's religion — particularly if that man has been dead for 225 years and was not in the habit of discussing his deepest convictions at any time during his life. Furthermore, there is a vast body of literature on the topic already in existence. The tiny stream which began around the middle of the nineteenth century with the publication of a few articles by the singer and conductor Johann Theodor Mosewius (1788–1858)[1] has swelled to such an extent in recent years that reviews of such publications have become full-length articles.[2] In addition to such specialized studies, the topic has been discussed in nearly all general accounts of the master's work for the past hundred years, having received the official sanction of the great Philipp Spitta (1841–1894). In view of all this, one might well ask whether any stone remains unturned.

Unfortunately, a great deal of this material is not helpful. Hundreds of pages have been devoted to discussing whether Bach was an orthodox Lutheran or a follower of Pietism.[3] When posed in such black-and-white terms, it is obvious that Bach could never

This paper was originally read prior to an organ recital of six Bach chorales played by Melville Cook, at McMaster University in October 1975.

have been a whole-hearted disciple of the latter, since in the words of Schweitzer:

> ...pietism was fundamentally inimical to art of any kind in worship, and was especially set against the concert style of the church music...So every cantor necessarily hated the pietists, and Bach took it particularly ill of them that they dragged his religious and artistic ideals in the dust.[4]

This is not to say, however, that the composer remained untouched by the Pietist movement; on the contrary, he seems to have been drawn toward certain elements within Pietism.[5] The point is, Bach would never have embraced some of the Pietist teachings and could not, therefore, have rejected Lutheran orthodoxy in favour of this particular theology.

There are problems, though, with the strict orthodox image. One of the difficulties with this interpretation is that it represents, for the most part, the opinion of writers who have themselves been conservative Lutherans. One has reason to suspect that some of the "conclusions" are less than entirely objective. All too often, information is ignored if it does not conform to the saintly image. Take, for instance, the frequently cited example of Hans Bach (1555–1615), an early member of that large contingent of musicians to come out of the Bach family. Of the two known pictures of this jolly figure, one bears the legend "Hans Back; morio celebris et facetus; fidicen ridiculus; homo laboriosus, simplex et pius"[6] — yet we are often told only that he was "industrious, simple and pious," as if those attributes were synonymous with the name Bach. What of his other attributes as "whimsical mischief-maker" and "ridiculous fiddler"? Are they not also part of the family tradition? Even the great master himself, according to C.P.E. Bach,[7] seems to have been involved in some youthful pranks — but we are not often reminded of that either.

Nevertheless, the scholarly consensus has been that Bach, theologically speaking, was essentially an orthodox Lutheran.[8] This judgment, though, poses something of a problem: can external dogma, no matter how deeply engrained, explain the creation of religious music of such power — music so marked by intensity and conviction?

Briefly, most of the conclusions about Bach's religious views have been based on the following evidence: a few documents of a public nature, the list of books from his library and, of course, the compositions themselves, particularly the church cantatas. Some of the public records show merely that Bach possessed the knowledge of church doctrine required of any church musician of his time; however, one early document sets forth a revealing professional goal: "a well-regulated church music, to the Glory of God."[9]

The inventory of Bach's estate lists some eighty-three volumes, all of which are concerned with religion in some way. This, to be sure, offers much potentially revealing information; indeed, the implications of this list have been discussed many times.[10] However, no one can claim to have read all of the works named in the inventory; in fact, a few of the titles are not known in any surviving copy today. Nevertheless, one of the most important items has just recently come to light — Bach's three-volume Bible with a commentary by the orthodox Lutheran theologian Abraham Calov (1612–1686). This work, now in the library of Concordia Seminary in St. Louis, contains various corrections of the text, several underlined passages, and even a few marginalia in Bach's own hand.[11]

These markings reveal Bach to have been a well-schooled student of the Bible, an informed layman with an unusually broad knowledge of theology and, above all else, a musician deeply concerned with the spiritual justification for his art. Most of the markings and observations are concerned with the commentary, rather than the text itself. Presumably, by the time he had acquired this work in 1733, Bach already knew the Bible text quite well, and was primarily interested in what Calov had to say about it. It will be some time before all the implications of this discovery can be worked out; however, a close study of Bach's Bible should help future scholarship.

Bach's church cantatas have often been cited as evidence of his personal beliefs. Considerable work has been done in this area, particularly with regard to the cantata texts.[12] The limitations of this line of investigation are rather obvious. First, the bulk of Bach's cantatas were written in the fairly brief span of three years; furthermore, most of these works were written as part of Bach's official duties and were intended for use in corporate worship services. Finally, Bach was often dealing with the words of other people; it is not at all clear how much control he had over the choice of the texts he set to music. Nevertheless, these studies have revealed a great deal about Bach's interpretive procedures, ranging from simple pictorialism to various degrees of abstract symbolism.[13]

Pictorialism, or "tone painting," is probably the most obvious of these procedures, since it often involves a direct allusion to the very words which are set to music. Because the use of tone painting is so closely associated with language, perhaps I can best illustrate the practice by citing a well-known example with an English text, such as the aria "Every Valley Shall Be Exalted" from Handel's *Messiah*. Calling to mind the melody for the words "the crooked straight," one can readily observe the way a Baroque composer might wish to "translate" a visual image into music. Bach's vocal works contain many examples of this common Baroque device; in fact, the references to the texts sometimes even assume the character of musical puns. For example, the "Sicut locutus est" from the *Magnificat* uses the music from the opening chorus and is thus musically "as it was in the beginning."

Another common concern of the Baroque composer was the representation of emotional states, according to an elaborate doctrine of "affections." Bach, like his contemporaries, believed that music could correctly represent feelings such as joy, sorrow, hatred or jealousy. This attitude was developed to the point that it even governed the choice of keys, since one key might express a desired "affect" more clearly than any other. (The key of D-major, for instance, is nearly always associated with a mood of festive joy.)

In Bach's music, even musical form can assume a symbolic meaning. Thus, a canon (Latin for "rule" or "law") might represent God's law (as in the first movement of Cantata 77), or an idea, such as following Christ (as in the bass aria "Ich folge Christo nach" from Canata 12). Naturally, the texts associated with these various other symbolic devices have helped to clarify the composer's intentions. Through the close study of such procedures in the vocal works, we have learned to recognize analogous symbolic gestures when they occur in the instrumental works.

One final area of Bach's symbolic language merits special consideration, because its intensely personal nature serves to illuminate some of the composer's innermost attitudes and convictions. I refer here to Bach's use of personal references and "signatures" in his music. The best-known of these is the B-A-C-H motive —

B-flat, A, C, B natural (which is called H in German nomenclature) — the most famous use of which occurs at the end of the final, unfinished fugue from the *Art of the Fugue*. In recent years, however, musicians have become increasingly aware that references to those pitches are hidden in quite a few of Bach's compositions. Even a thrice-familiar work like the chorus "Jesu, Joy of Man's Desiring" from Cantata 147 can contain direct quotations of the motive which somehow manage to slip past undetected (see Example I).

Example I

This passage is not easily dismissed as "mere coincidence," since it occurs exactly two-thirds of the way through the composition; furthermore, the high C in the first B-A-C-H is the highest note in the entire movement.

Since World War II it has been established that Bach sometimes resorted to a cabalistic number alphabet, by which means he was able to introduce numerical signatures into his compositions. It had been known for some time that Bach had employed number symbolism in some of his compositions. At times, the symbolism involved little more than numerical tone painting (ten for the commandments, three for the Trinity, etc.); in some cases, though, it seemed that the composer had used numbers to refer to more abstract concepts (for example, proportions) or even to certain biblical passages, particularly the Psalms.

After the war, the German theologian and Bach scholar, Friedrich Smend, presented a convincing case for Bach's use of gematria.[14] After pointing to evidence proving the existence of gematria among Bach's colleagues, Smend went to on to show how the signature numbers of 14 ($B+A+C+H = 2+1+3+8$) and 41 ($J=9$; $S=18$; $9+18+14 = 41$) were used in several different compositions. Perhaps Smend's best illustration was the chorale prelude "Vor deinen Thron tret' ich" (*BWV* 668), which, we are told, Bach dictated from his death bed. In this work, the chorale melody appears as a *cantus firmus* in the soprano voice (see Example II).

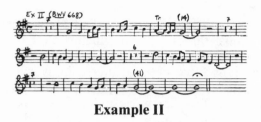

Example II

It can be seen that only the first phrase of the melody is orna-
mented, while the remainder of the chorale is presented in a simple undecorated form. Smend pointed out that the decorated
phrase contains 14 notes, which, in combination with the remaining notes, produce the other signature number of 41 for the entire
cantus firmus. The meaning is clear: on his death bed, the composer is able to proclaim that he, Bach — J.S. Bach — is ready to
stand before the throne of God. Smend noted also that the title
chosen by the composer was not the usual text for the chorale
melody; however, Bach's title is a vital key to understanding the
personal significance of the composition.

An interesting parallel to Bach's last chorale prelude can be
seen in an apparently early work, the prelude on "Valet will ich
dir geben" (*BWV* 736), which deals with the subject of death in a
far more exuberant manner than the work discussed above. Here,
the "festive" key of D-major is confirmed by an energetic triplet
figure in the manual parts. In this work, the *cantus firmus* is
assigned to the pedals, where it is sounded in majestic long notes.
Once again, though, the chorale melody is presented in 41 written
notes;[15] moreover, it is probably no accident that the *fourteenth*
note is the only shortened note (shortened to allow for the only
ornamental passing tone).

Numerical signatures often occur in conjunction with B-A-C-H
motives in a kind of "double" signature. Referring back to Example I, we can now see that the 14 notes between the two melodic
signatures doubtlessly represent a third reference to the name
Bach.[16] Both melodic and numerical signatures can be found in
virtually every type of composition. Even an apparently free,
improvisatory work, such as the famous D-minor *Toccata con
Fuga* (*BWV* 565), can contain amazingly elaborate numerical patterns. In that composition, the signature numbers 14 and 41 are
presented in combination with various kinds of threes. It would
seem that this numerical "theme" is given even in the title (3

words and 14 letters) and in the total number of measures (143).

From the commanding 14-note motive with which the work opens to the final resounding chord, there is scarcely a single note which is not related to one of the basic numbers. Space does not permit a complete discussion of the numerical scheme; however, I might, in passing, call attention to the first three pedal notes — all three are low Ds (a pitch which is eventually sounded 14 times). Furthermore, by the end of the third pedal note (m. 12), a total of 333 notes have sounded in all parts. We might also notice the 41 pedal notes in the last 14 measures of the composition, and the cadenzas of 14 and 33 notes in the toccata.

The real *tour de force*, however, takes place in the final seven measures of the composition. Beginning with the first beat of measure 137, Bach sets up a pattern of alternating five-note chords and five-note arpeggios which continues without interruption for 14 beats, at which point (m. 140!) the pattern is broken by the introduction of a six-note chord. The 149 notes $(1 + 4 + 9 = 14)$ contained in the entire seven measures is thus sub-divided into two perfect squares $(100 + 49)$, both of which have prime factors which add to 14. Finally, reading backwards from the line of division, we discover a retrograde B-A-C-H which is hammered out in exactly 14 eighth notes (see Example III).

Ex. III (BWV 565)

Example III

Perhaps number symbolism, as the most hidden aspect of Bach's musical language, offers the greatest potential for insight into the composer's deepest and most personal convictions. It should be remembered that historically the practice was always a secret art, and that it was often used for the expression of religious ideas, particularly by the Pythagoreans and by the Jewish mystics.[17] In combination with the other modes of symbolic expression, it seems possible that Bach may have left a fairly complete record of his religious experience simply by the control of numerical patterns in his music. It remains for us to attempt to locate and interpret these hidden patterns. For this purpose I propose a closer examination of the symbolic content of a representative group of organ compositions.

It should be noted that the above-mentioned limitations of the cantatas as evidence of the composer's view do not apply to the compositions for organ. Bach's organ works span his entire career as a composer, from some of the earliest works (where he seems to have been teaching himself to perform as well as compose) right up to his very last composition, which, as we have seen, he dictated from his death bed. Furthermore, the bulk of his effort in this area was not a requisite of his employment. For the last thirty-three years of his life, his duties did not even include organ playing. We know that by this time he was a master of improvisation; it would not have been necessary, therefore, for him to write out pieces for his own use as a recitalist.

In this connection, we might recall that Bach's immediate ancestors were not organists or, for that matter, even church musicians. His decision to master the instrument seems to have been a matter of personal choice rather than family tradition. It is possible that this decision, which he probably made in his early teens, represented an orientation towards the world of sacred music. The organ had already acquired a role as the "God-praising instrument," associated with the sacred rather than the secular. Bach was certainly astute enough to realize, as did the young Handel, that opera was the glittering pinnacle of the Baroque musical world. However, he never wrote an opera, although, as court composer, he surely could have had one produced in Dresden, had he so desired.

That many of Bach's organ works represent volitional efforts on his part can scarcely be doubted; however, it has been suggested that the composer expected to reap a financial reward from the works he brought to press. I doubt it. The title page of the *Clavier-Übung*, Part III, the longest of the published collections for organ, suggests that Bach was well aware of the rather limited market for these esoteric pieces, since he addresses himself to "music lovers" and particularly to "connoisseurs of such work"

(Kennern von dergleichen Arbeit). In all likelihood, Bach himself helped to engrave this work, probably in an attempt to reduce expenses on a venture which stood to lose, rather than to gain, financially.

Bach's title pages also provide good evidence — the most direct we have — of his purpose in writing for the organ. His objectives are expressed quite clearly in the little dedication rhyme from the *Orgelbüchlein*:

> *Dem Höchsten Gott allein zu Ehren,*
> *dem Nechsten draus sich zu belehren*
> (To the praise of God, alone Most High,
> and for the instruction of those nearby)

In addition, many of Bach's scores bear the heading "J. J." (Jesu Juva — Jesus help me), while at the end, he offers God the glory with the letters "S. D. Gl." (*Soli Deo Gloria*). These gestures tend to suggest a deep spiritual commitment; however, they could be dismissed as meaningless habits or even "window dressing" were it not for the internal evidence offered by so many of the compositions, particularly the chorale preludes.

Instead of discussing individual works at random I shall limit my remarks to one unified set of chorale preludes, the *Sechs Chorale* (*Six Chorales*), which merit particular attention since they were published some time between 1746 and Bach's death in 1750, having been engraved by one of the composer's former students, Johann Georg Schübler of Zella.[18] (The fact that five of the six movements also appear in cantatas dating from 1724 to 1731 should be mentioned; however, it is not a primary concern here.)

The underlying unity of the six pieces can be grasped fairly simply by reading the texts of the chorales in sequence. Ideally, all of the verses of each hymn should be taken into account, but the basic ideas can be demonstrated by the first verses alone. (The texts will be found immediately following this article.) In the opening chorale, Christ is depicted in the mystical role of the bridegroom about to enter the benighted world, represented by the city of Jerusalem. In the second chorale, however, we see that the imminence of the Saviour is the cause of acute anxiety for the person who is not prepared to go forth to meet the bridegroom. The awareness of the sinful condition gives rise to a misery which cannot be assuaged by anything in the world. ("Whither shall I flee.")

The third chorale provides the answer to the question posed by the second: Trust God, hope in Him always; His love will sustain, come what may. Once God has become the true guide, the redeemed soul lifts his voice in a hymn of praise, in the fourth chorale.The fifth chorale, "Ach bleib bei uns," is in effect a prayer for strength and comfort at the end of life. The final composition, then, looks beyond death to the second coming, when heaven and earth will be united. It should be noted that this text, the one indicated by Bach's title, is not well known; in fact, it seems to have been obscure in Bach's own day, since it does not occur in any of his vocal compositions. What Bach has presented, therefore, is a theologically inspired Christian life cycle, the key to which is to be discovered by a careful reading of the words associated with the chorale melodies as indicated by Bach's own titles.

To be sure, the cyclical element can be interpreted at other levels, ranging from daily renewal through the annual (for example, the liturgical themes of Advent) to the eternal. The eschatological theme, which appears so often in Bach's works,[19] is very much in evidence here and, as usual, is open to various interpretations. Nevertheless, the basic concept of cyclic order is operative at all levels and is, in fact, reinforced by such structural details as the sequence of keys and the placement of the chorale melodies.[20]

Many aspects of this plan are apparent in the musical settings Bach has provided for the chorales, ranging from simple pictorialism to somewhat more abstract devices. A good example of the former can be found in the fifth of the chorales, where the "true light" of the Word seems to be represented by the placement of the unornamented *cantus firmus* high in the right hand. The other two parts sometimes reflect the light (by quoting small segments of the *cantus firmus*), while the rapid runs and leaps of the left hand seem to depict the flickering shadows at the edge of the darkness.[21]

A somewhat similar device can be observed in the second chorale, where the counterpoint aptly depicts the nervous scurrying to and fro in a futile search for relief. Nevertheless, Bach did offer an alternate title for this composition: "Auf meinen lieben Gott," a text which expresses trust in the God of love. It can hardly be doubted that the composition depicts the anxiety of the first text, rather than the trust of the second. Perhaps what is intended here is a silent reminder that God is ever present, even in the depths of despair. In the words of this second text:

Mein Unglück kann er wenden:
Steht all's in seinen Händen.
(He can turn my misfortune around:
Everything is in His Hands.)

And of course, the "extra" words of the alternate title fit rather handily into a little numerical game Bach plays with titles in this work: the addition of these four words to the German titles of the other six pieces produces a total of forty-one words, in answer to the fourteen words of the collective title:[22]

SECHS CHORALE
von verschiedener Art
auf einer
Orgel
mit 2 Clavieren und Pedal
vorzuspielen
"Wachet auf rufft uns die Stimme"
"Wo soll ich fliehen hin" ("Auf meinen lieben Gott")
"Wer nur den lieben Gott laesst walten"
"Meine seele erhebt den Herren"
"Ach bleib bey uns Herr Jesu Christ"
"Komst du nun Jesu vom Himmel herunter"
[14 = B A C H; 41 = J. S. B A C H]

Bach's compositional procedures also tend to reflect his interpretation of the texts. Particularly instructive is the contrast between the second and third chorale preludes regarding the relationship between the *cantus firmus* and the other parts. In both works, the chorale melody is placed in the pedal, sounding an octave higher than notated. In "Wo soll ich fliehen hin," the two manual voices are completely independent of the chorale;[23] rather, they imitate each other, following, as it were, the fleeting ways of the world. Exactly opposite is the case in the following composition, in which all three manual voices are based directly on the *cantus firmus*, in a musical demonstration of the admonition of the text: allow God to be your guide; build on Him.

A somewhat less literal procedure is followed in the two outer pieces, "Wachet auf" and "Kommst du nun." In both pieces the combination of dance rhythms and major keys combine to produce an atmosphere of joy and confidence. In the first chorale, the three completely independent melodic lines, which move along together in harmony, may be a representation of the Holy Trinity. Certainly, there seem to be other Trinitarian elements in force here, ranging from the key signature (E-flat major) to the three repeated pedal notes at the outset, and even the arrangement of the music in the original edition (pages 1 to 3!): three pages, with three lines of score on each page, and three staves in each line.

The theologically informed observer will no doubt be interested to learn that the chorale upon which this first prelude is based was written by Philipp Nicolai (1556–1608); it was published in 1599, along with Nicolai's other great hymn "Wie schon leichtet der Morgenstern," as an appendix to the author's famous *Freudenspiegel des ewigen Lebens*.[24] Is Bach drawing on the associations of Nicolai's name? Concepts such as mystical union with Christ, the indwelling of the Trinity, spiritual rebirth and an experiential relationship to God are, according to F. Ernest Stoeffler, some of the basic themes of Nicolai's theological writings.[25] As we have seen, such ideas are not at all foreign to the overall scheme of the *Six Chorales*.

Of the six compositions, though, the one which offers the greatest challenge interpretively is the prelude on the Magnificat, "Meine Seele erhebt den Herren" (*BWV* 648). The text is Luther's translation of the Virgin's canticle of praise. Yet Bach's setting is permeated with the kind of chromaticism most often associated with sorrow or grief. This approach, which runs counter to the doctrine of the "affections," seems to indicate a rather subjective interpretation. It should come as no surprise that the B-A-C-H motive is woven into the very fabric of the intricate counterpoint. The clearest presentation of signature occurs at measures 7 and 8 where the tenor and alto lines *cross*. (See Example IV.) This point is, by the way, the numerical centre of the entire set of six pieces, if the measures are numbered according to the original edition.

Example IV

Perhaps the enigma can never be resolved entirely. However, there seems to be an important numerical clue presented by the unaccompanied pedal theme with which the composition opens and closes. (Note that this is the only monophonic passage in the entire collection.) The 22 notes of this ritornello theme are probably a reference to Psalm 22 — the famous "passion" psalm quoted by Christ just before his death.[26] ("My God, my God, why hast thou forsaken me?" [Ps. 22:1]. The anguish of the soul who feels so alone is intensified by the mockings of those around him.) Yet out of all this despair, there suddenly arises a hymn of praise: "I will declare thy name unto my brethren: in the midst of the congregation will I praise thee" (Ps. 22:22). This is precisely what happens in Bach's chorale prelude. The *cantus firmus*, carrying with it the positive affirmation of the silent text, rises out of the grief-laden counterpoint. Bach's treatment strongly suggests that, even though there is much suffering to be endured in this vale of tears, the redeemed soul can still proclaim God's dominion over all. From what we know of the composer's life, the sentiments might well derive from personal experience. Bach had certainly experienced rejection and a great deal of personal sorrow (after all, he lost his first wife and carried eleven of those twenty children to their graves).

The reference to Psalm 22 may also represent an uncommonly profound interpretation of Mary's role as the lowly handmaid of the Lord. The setting suggests that her decision to become the instrument of divine will has been made with the knowledge that it will entail much personal sorrow and even ridicule. Similar ideas are developed in the *Compendium locorum theologicorum* of Leonard Hutter — a work which Hans Besch sees as a key to a theological understanding of Bach's religion. A principal point of that work, according to Besch, is the image of the prophets and the apostles as the tools of divine inspiration.[27] (One is reminded here of the visual representations of the apostles and even St. Gregory in which they are seen working with the Holy Spirit whispering directly into their ears.) This concept has been cited by Gerhard Herz as part of the self-image of a tragic figure well aware of his own genius.[28] Perhaps, as I have suggested elsewhere, Bach was able to endure much pain because of his conviction that, as the chosen instrument of the Holy Spirit, he was allowed to participate in the ongoing process of creation.[29] In all humility, he may have felt that he had received a power greater than his own, and that this power enabled him to testify to the glory of God until the end of the earth (Luke 24). This kind of eschatological hope is implied in both the psalm and the Magnificat texts.

As a set of pieces, the *Six Chorales* offer a great deal of insight into the religious views Bach seems to have held near the end of life. The evidence is mostly symbolic, and symbols are, by their nature, general rather than exact: they tend to point at truths too profound and too subtle for the restricted vocabulary of ordinary language. Nevertheless, the basic idea seems clear enough: all life proceeds from a Triune Source, and with the help of God's guidance there can be an eventual return to the joy-filled realm of the Spirit; the path might at times be difficult, but faith and the light of God's Word help to make the journey bearable.

Most of these ideas are clearly set forth in the teachings of Nicolai concerning the concept of vivification, or spiritual rebirth, the seven-fold plan which, in Stoeffler's words, encompasses "justification [by Faith], adoption, spiritual marriage, indwelling of God, elevation to royal priesthood, renewal of the spirit and the divine trial of the Christian. [Nicolai felt that] after... rebirth man has returned to his original state in which he is indwelt by the Trinity and permeated by the heavenly life. In this state eternal life is the present possession of the baptized believer and will, of course, be his forever."[30]

Despite the pronounced mystical element, these are not the ideas of an unorthodox reformer, but an echo of concepts articulated hundreds of years ago by St. Paul in his discourse on life after death (I Corinthians 15). This chapter is, I believe, of the greatest importance to our understanding of Bach's religion and goes a long way towards helping us to understand the composer's apparent longing for death. Like Paul, Bach probably "experienced" death often: "I die daily," said Paul (I Cor 15:30).

Bach would probably also join the apostle "born out of due time" in proclaiming:

> By the grace of God I am what I am: and his grace which was bestowed on me was not in vain; but I laboured more abundantly than they all: yet not I, but the grace of God which was with me. (I Cor. 15:10)

The theme of mystical encounter has come up repeatedly in

these remarks; however, I am not trying to resurrect Schweitzer's contention that "Bach's real religion was not orthodox Lutheranism, but mysticism."[31] On the other hand, I do not reject it to the extent some have, claiming it lacks the grace and insight for which the beloved doctor was known.

The problem with Schweitzer's remark is that mysticism as I understand the term is not a religion, but an experience. It ought not be contrasted with a structured religion. As William James pointed out in 1902, one of the most striking features of the experience is its ineffability: "The subject of it immediately says that it defies expression, that no adequate report of its contents can be given in words."[32] And yet, these experiences usually generate a strong conviction that they are of great importance and contain the seeds of ultimate truth; and "as a rule they carry with them a curious sense of authority for after-time."[33]

The great Jewish scholar and expert on mysticism, Gershom G. Scholem, while agreeing with what James had to say, has delineated some of the reasons why this shattering experience very often has an extremely conservative expression:

> The moment a mystic tries to clarify his experience by
> reflection. . . especially when he attempts to commu-
> nicate it to others, he cannot help imposing a frame-
> work of conventional symbols and ideas upon it. . . .
> the mystic's experience tends to confirm the religious
> authority under which he lives; its theology and sym-
> bols are projected into his mystical experience, but
> do not spring from it.[34]

Scholem then proceeds to emphasize the importance of symbols and holy texts to the mystic, for it is through these that the mystic strives to uncover new levels of meaning within his own tradition. With this in mind, it is easy to see how the Bible came to play such an important role in Bach's religious life. Referring back to the *Six Chorales* for a moment, we can see a specific reference to the gospel text (Luke 24:29) which is quoted in the title of the fifth prelude, "Ach bleib bei uns" ("Abide with us"). The biblical passage in which this phrase appears concerns the events at Emmaus, where the risen Christ appeared and "opened the Scriptures" to two of the disciples. This is the kind of illumination of which Nicolai wrote and which many mystics have described — a magical moment when all conflicts are resolved. Some even seem to feel a sense of cosmic order and harmony at such moments of revelation.

The word "cosmic," by the way, is Pythagorean in origin. Pythagoras himself was a mystic, who found in music and numbers the symbols he used to express his vision of universal harmony. This tradition was picked up by the early church fathers, particularly St. Augustine, who attempted to explain biblical passages containing numbers according to Pythagorean concepts.[35] Seen in this light, Bach's use of numbers is part of a long tradition of mystical expression — a tradition which was beginning to die out in Bach's own lifetime, although, as we have seen, it was still known and practised in Bach's close circle of friends. However, the secret nature of the Pythagorean concepts remained part of the symbolism.

The impression we get from assembling the various kinds of evidence available — direct, implied and symbolic — is that Bach's religious stance was essentially that of an orthodox Lutheran of his day; however, it was not the dry dogma and meaningless rhetoric about which the reformers of the period complained. By means of profound personal experience — "mysticism," for lack of a better word — he was able to breathe new life into the old formulas. In the words of Gerhard Herz, "Bach clung to the old because it was not yet old to him."[36]

It seems to me that an awareness of the ideas and symbolic language Bach would have known opens up areas of Bach's work which lie outside our ordinary perception of music. The composer stands at the dividing line between two musical worlds. There is a Janus-faced aspect to his art; it is only natural that we should understand the face turned towards the future better than that which faces the past. For modern man, the primary meaning of his music will remain in its purely musical, esthetic qualities; these are what we find so moving — even compelling — in his work. This does not mean, however, that we cannot become aware of a different kind of symbolic "content" in Bach's music. To me, the exploration of some of these layers of meaning is one of the things which makes even the most familiar pieces remain interesting. We can never be sure that the last Chinese box has been opened.

Randolph Currie

TEXTS FOR THE CHORALE MELODIES SET BY BACH
IN HIS SIX CHORALES

1.

Wachet auf! ruft uns die
Stimme
Der Wächter sehr hoch auf der
Zinne:
Wach auf, du Stadt Jerusalem!
Mitternacht heisst diese Stunde!
Sie rufen uns mit hellem
Munde:
Wo seid ihr klugen Jungfrauen,
Wohl auf, der Bräut'gam
kommt!
Steht auf, die Lampen nehmt!
Hallelujah!
Macht euch bereit
Zu der Hochzeit:
Ihr müsset ihm entgegen gehn.

1.

Wake, awake, for night is
flying,
The watchmen on the heights
are crying:
Awake, Jerusalem, at last!
Midnight hears the welcome
voices,
And at the thrilling cry rejoices;
Come forth, ye virgins, night is
past!
The Bridegroom comes, awake,
Your lamps with gladness take;
Alleluia!
And for his marriage feast
prepare,
For ye must go to meet Him
there.
—Tr. by Catherine Winkworth,
(1829-78)

2.

Wo soll ich fliehen hin,
Weil ich beschweret bin
Mit viel und grossen Sünden
Wo kann ich Rettung finden?
Wenn alle Welt herkäme:
Mein Angst sie nicht
    wegnähme.

2.

O whither shall I flee,
Depressed with misery?
Who is it that can ease me,
And from my sins release me?
Man's help I vain have proved,
Sin's load remains unmoved.
—Tr. Anon, Moravian
Hymn-Book, 1754

3.

Wer nur den lieben Gott lässt
    walten
Und hoffet auf ihn allezeit,
Den wird er wunderlich erhalten
In aller Noth und Traurigkeit
Wer Gott, dem Allerhöchsten,
    traut,
Der hat auf keinen Sand gebaut.

3

If thou but suffer God to guide
    thee,
And hope in Him through all
    thy ways,
He'll give thee strength, what'er
    betide thee,
And bear thee through the evil
    days;
Who trusts in God's unchanging
    love
Builds on the rock that nought
    can move.
—Tr. by Catherine Winkworth,

4.

Meine Seel' erhebt den Herren
Und mein Geistfreut sich
   Gottes, meines Heilands.

4.

My soul doth magnify the Lord,
And my spirit hath rejoiced in
   God my saviour. (King James
   Bible)

5.

Ach bleib bei uns, Herr Jesu
   Christ,
Weil es nun Abend worden ist:
Dein Wort, O Herr, das ewig
   Licht,
Lass ja bei uns auslöschen nicht.

5.

Lord Jesus Christ, with us
   abide,
For now, behold 'tis eventide:
And bring, to cheer us thro' the
   night,
Thy Word, our true and only
   light.

       —Tr. by Benjamin Hall
       Kennedy, 1863.

6.

Kommst du nun, Jesu, von
   Himmel herunter auf Erden?
Soll nun der Himmel und Erde
   vereiniget werden?
Ewiger Gott,
Kann dich mein Jammer und
   Not
Bringen zu Menschengebärden?

6.

Art Thou, Lord Jesus, from
heaven to
earth now descending?
Shall now the earth with high
heaven in
union be blending?
Eternal God,
Can all my need and my woe
Bring Thee as man, Thy help
lending?
—Tr. H.H. [Helen Hewitt]

Notes

1. Mendelssohn's performance of the *Saint Matthew Passion* in 1829 seems to have stimulated the interest of Mosewius in the subject of Bach's religion. Two of the Bach articles were reprinted separately: *J.S. Bach in seinen Kirchencantaten und Choralgesängen* (1845) and *J.S. Bachs Matthäus Passion* (1852). See *Baker's Biographical Dictionary of Musicians*, 5th ed. (New York, 1971), s.v. "Mosewius."

2. For a thorough survey of the literature on Bach theology up to 1945, see Hans Besch, *J.S. Bach: Frömmigkeit und Glaube*, 2nd ed. (Kassel, 1950), vol. 1. Since that time, publications in the field have been reviewed most satisfactorily in a series of brilliant articles by Walter Blankenburg. See particularly, "Theologische und geistesgeschichtliche Probleme der gegenwärtigen Bachforschung," *Theologische Literaturzeitung* 78 (1953), and "Zwölf Jahre Bachforschung," *Acta Musicologica* 37 (1965).

3. For a typical orthodox interpretation, see Wilibald Gurlitt, *J.S. Bach, the Master and his Works* (St. Louis: Concordia, 1957), pp. 75-81. On the other hand, Erik Routley has assumed a strong influence of Pietism on Bach in *Church Music and Theology* (Philadelphia: Muhlenberg, 1959), pp. 46-50.

4. Albert Schweitzer, *J.S. Bach*, trans. Ernest Newman (New York, 1911), 1:169.

5. The element of mysticism, particularly, along with the Pietists' emphasis on emotion and the authority of the Bible, seems likely to have had a strong appeal for Bach as he grew older. Karl Geiringer cites "a mystic undercurrent" in many of the cantata texts chosen by Bach (which was strengthened by his intense musical settings) as bringing those works "perilously close" to the controversial teachings of Pietism. See *Johann Sebastian Bach: The Culmination of an Era* (New York, 1966), p. 151.

6. The engraving, dated 1617, is reproduced by Karl Geiringer in *The Bach Family: Seven Generations of Creative Genius* (New York, 1954), plate IV, facing p. 32.

7. Mentioned in a letter to Bach's first biographer, J.N. Forkel (1749-1818). See Hans T. David and Arthur Mendle, eds., *The Bach Reader*, rev. ed. (New York, 1966), p. 277.

8. That Bach did hold sincere religious convictions of *some* sort has seldom been doubted; however, a few years ago, one leading scholar, Friedrich Blume, did question the depth of Bach's commitment to his faith in "Outlines of a New Picture of Bach," *Music and Letters* 44: 214 ff. Since the storm of protest over Blume's ideas has finally died down, I do not wish to raise the issue again. Although essentially incorrect, Blume did raise some valid objections, particularly concerning some of the overly enthusiastic writers who had erected a saintly image of Bach. Some of Blume's objections about the use of the cantatas as evidence of Bach's personal beliefs are, I feel, well taken; therefore, the discussion of the cantatas in this paper includes some of his reservations along with some of my own.

9. David and Mendle, *Bach Reader*, p. 60; see also p. 93. The original German of these and other relevant documents is reproduced by Werner Neuman and Hans-Joachim Schulze, eds., in *Bach-Dokumente*, 1. (Kassel, 1963-69). The passage quoted here is from a petition dated 25 June 1708.

10. Bach's theological books are listed in chap. 9 of his estate; see Neuman and Schulze, *Dokumente* 2:494-96; and David and Mendle, *Bach Reader*, pp. 95 ff. Further information is given in H. Preus, *Bachs Bibliothek* (Leipzig, 1928), reprinted from *Zahn-Festausgabe*. For the most complete discussion of the implications to date, see Besch, *J.S. Bach*. A study of the Lutheran books in Bach's library by Anglican theologian and music scholar Robin A. Leaver is scheduled for publication in the 1975 *Bach-Jahrbuch*; however, the article was not available at the time of this publication.

11. For a description of Bach's Bible and a transcription of the marginal notations, see Christoph Trautmann, "Calovii Schrifften. 3 Bände," *Musik und Kirche* 39, no. 4 (1969). In a somewhat abbreviated English translation by Hilton Oswald, this article is also available in the *Concordia Theological Monthly* 42, no. 2 (1971).

12. For the texts themselves, see Werner Neumann, *J.S. Bach: Sämtliche Kantatentexte* (Leipzig, 1956); for a thorough discussion of one aspect of the subject, see Roy A. Reed, Jr., "Spenerian Pietism and the Cantatas of Johann Sebastian Bach" Ph. D. diss., Boston University, 1968.

13. Concerning symbolism in general, the most important single work is Arnold Schering's collection of articles entitled *Das Symbol in der Musik* (Leipzig, 1941). An excellent essay on the subject as it pertains to Bach's clavier works is included in Erwin Bodkey, *The Interpretation of Bach's Keyboard Works* (Cambridge, Mass., 1960), pp. 223-58.

14. The word "gematria" refers specifically to the "practice of assigning numerical values to the letters of the alphabet." (Vincent Foster Hopper, *Medieval Number Symbolism* [New York, 1938], p. 62.)

According to Smend, Bach's gematria uses the 24 letters of the Roman alphabet as follows: A = 1, B = 2, etc.; I and J = 9; U and V = 20. (See F. Smend, *J.S. Bach: Kirchen-Kantaten* [Berlin, 1947-49], vols. 5,6.)

Prior to Smend's discovery of Bach's use of the number alphabet, the most complete discussion of Bach's use of number symbolism was Martin Jansen's article, "Bach Zahlen-Symbolik, an seinen Passionen untersucht," *Bach-Jahrbuch* (1937), p. 96 ff.

15. Note, however, that the first 13 notes of the *cantus firmus* are enclosed in repeat signs and thus are heard twice in the performance. This reservation does not apply, though, in the case of *BWV* 668. Bach may have lines from verse 3 in mind in making this setting:

> In meines Herzens Grunde
> Dein Nam und Kreuz allein
> Funkelt all Zeit und Stunde:
> Drauf kan ich fröhlich sein.

16. Apparently, the form of the entire movement is governed by numerical considerations, since the body of the movement, exclusive of the framing ritornels, can be thought of as 41 + 14 measures; notice that the two sections are bridged by the second of the two B-A-C-H quotations (m. 49-50). The entire pattern, then, is:

Section:	Ritornel —	(41-meas. unit) —	(14 meas. unit) —	Ritornel
		B-A-C-H		
Measures:	1-8	9-49	50-63	64-71

17. For a brief historical background of the use of numerology, see Hopper, *Number Symbolism*, and Christopher Butler, *Number Symbolism* (New York, 1970).

18. J.G. Schubler (c. 1720-?) also engraved most of the *Musical Offering*, which is securely dated 1747. For a more complete discussion of the origins and publication of the collection, see my article, "Cyclic Unity in Bach's 'Sechs Chorale,'" *Bach* 4, nos. 1, 2 (1973).

19. The strong eschatological emphasis in Bach's vocal works is pointed up by William H. Scheide in *Johann Sebastian Bach as a Biblical Interpreter* (Princeton, 1952), p. 18. Many writers have discussed Bach's apparent "longing for death" without mentioning the complex theological implications of the subject.

20. See my "Cyclic Unity," part 1, pp. 27-30. Briefly, there are three pairs of chorales, which are linked together by keys a major third apart; further, these same three groups are also related by the *cantus firmus* placement — 2 and 3 (in the pedal at 4, pitch), 4 and 5 (in the R.H.) and 1 and 6 (in the L.H.)

21. The imagery of the chorale text itself is based on Luke 24:28-32, a passage which may have had great personal significance for Bach.

22. The orthography used here is that of the original edition. The title page of the first edition is reproduced in facsimile in Georg Kinsky, *Die Originalausgaben der Werke Johann Sebastian Bachs* (Vienna, 1937), p. 58, and in my article, "Cyclic Unity."

23. Thematically independent counterpoint is rare in Bach's chorale preludes and usually exists "for special reasons," according to Hermann Keller, *The Organ Works of Bach*, trans. Helen Hewitt (New York, 1967), p. 243.

24. The two hymns, the only chorales ever written by Nicolai, were added to the author's *Freudenspiegel* in gratitude for having survived a disastrous plague in 1597. (See facsimile reprint [Soest, 1963], p. 409 ff.) The texts of both chorales contain acrostics in honour of Wilhelm Ernst, Count of Graf, a student of Nicolai's, who died in 1598 at the age of fifteen. (See C.S. Terry, *Bach's Chorales* [London, 1919] 2:405.)

25. F. Ernest Stoeffler, "The Rise of Evangelical Pietism," in *Studies in the History of Religions* (Leiden, 1965), 9:197ff.

26. J.E. Funing-Jurgens has suggested that the structural uses of the number 22 in Obrecht's Good Friday motet *Parce Domine* likewise constitute a hidden reference to the passion psalm. He points out that the number of notes in the motet is equal to the number of words in the original Hebrew text, 253, a number which turns out to be the sum of all the numbers from 1 to 22. (He further observes that the Hebrew text has 1,012 letters, or 4 X 253.) See "More About Jacob Obrecht's Parce Domine,' " *Tijdschrift van de Verenging voor Neder-landse Muziekgeschiedenis* 21 (1970), p. 177. The elaborate numerical constructs in Obrecht's motet suggest that perhaps numerical composition in music was highly developed over 200 years before Bach's day, while the patterns in the Hebrew seem to indicate a very ancient artistic tradition, indeed. (The number 22 was a favourite structural factor among the Old Testament poets, probably because of the 22 letters of the Hebrew alphabet.)

27. Besch, *J.S. Bach*, p. 239. Although dating from 1610, Hutter's *Compendium* was still used as a basis for religious instruction when Bach was a student in Ohrdruf and Lüneburg.

28. Gerhard Herz, "Toward a New Image of Bach," *BACH* 2, no. 1, (1971): 27.

29. Randolph Currie, "A Neglected Guide to Bach's Use of Number Symbolism," BACH 5 (1974); see particularly pp. 28 ff, and p. 9.

30. Stoeffler, "The Rise of Evangelical Pietism," p. 199.

31. Schweitzer, *J.S. Bach*, p. 169.

32. William James, *The Varieties of Religious Experience* (New York, 1963; first printed in 1902), p. 380.

33. *Ibid.* The term "mysticism" is used here exactly as James described it. It does *not* refer to a codified system of theology, although "Mystic Ways" have been certainly formulated. Even within orthodox Lutheranism a few rigidly defined mystic doctrines were formulated, most importantly, the concept of the *unio mystica* (see Wolfgang Herbst, *Johann Sebastian Bach und die lutherische*

Mystik, published by the author at Chemnitz ?, c. 1958). The problem with nearly all doctrines about mystical interludes is that they tend to put a strait jacket of words on an experience that can only be described in very general terms, if at all. One recent attempt at defining the phenomenon, however, is perhaps instructive: "... they are episodes of intense and immediate cognition in which the total personality of a person is absorbed in an intimate though transient relationship with the basic forces, cycles and mechanisms at work in the universe and in his own psychosomatic composite — gravity, cosmic rays, light, heat, electromagnetism, cycles of breathing, circulation, digestion, day, year, life, death." (Andrew M. Greeley and William C. McCready, "Are We a Nation of Mystics?" *New York Times Magazine*, 26 Jan. 1975, p. 23.) The authors report that the respondents to their survey tended to be "*creative*, happy, dynamic... [and constructively] *intense*" (p. 22, my italics).

34. Gershom G. Scholem, *On the Kabbalah and its Symbolism*, trans. Ralph Manheim (New York, 1965), p. 8 ff.

35. See note 17 above. Concerning the "mystical" nature of classical numerology, see Gunnar Qvarnström, *Poetry and Numbers: On the Structural Use of Symbolic Numbers* (Lund, 1966), pp. 17-25. The author apparently has a rather limited view of mysticism, for he fails to see how the highly rational manipulation of numbers could, in fact, be used to express a mystical experience. He does, however, see Bach's use of numbers as part of the intellectual tradition dating back to Pythagoras by way of St. Augustine and the *Numerorum mysteria* of Petrus Bongus (1585).

36. Gerhard Herz, "Bach's Religion," *Journal of Renaissance and Baroque Music* 1, no. 2 (1946): 137.

The Jansenists and the Enlightenment in France

The traditional view of the relationship between the Jansenists and the Enlightenment in France stresses the opposition between the Jansenists and the *philosophes*. The tendency towards a pessimistic world view in Pascal is contrasted with the more optimistic outlook of Voltaire. The consistent hostility of the editor of the Jansenist paper, *Les Nouvelles ecclésiastiques*, to the *philosophes* was well known to contemporaries. And eighteenth-century writers, such as the Marquis d'Argenson, the journalist Barbier, Voltaire and D'Alembert, made much of the paradox of the Jansenists, furthering the cause of the *philosophes* and Enlightenment by stirring up division and turmoil in the Church, creating a distaste for religion and distracting the censorship authorities.

In recent years the traditional view has been undergoing some revision from two directions. First, more attention is being given to the weaknesses of what some French historians, such as Louis Trénard, have been calling a too Manichean approach to the Enlightenment, an approach in which the polarities between good and evil, between enlightened and non-enlightened, are drawn too closely and too precisely. The social history of the *Ancien Régime* is now more closely allied with its intellectual history, as seen, for example, in Daniel Roche's study of the French provincial academies and the diffusion of the Enlightenment. Groups that were formerly regarded as outside or on the fringes of Enlightened thought are understood as perhaps having had more in common with the *philosophes* than was once thought. Second, the Jansenism of the eighteenth century is now better understood and seen as more than a degenerate form of the original theological and religious reform movement, largely given over to political activities.

The author wishes to thank the Canada Council for assistance in conducting the research that this paper is based on.

This would seem to be, therefore, an appropriate time to question again the relationship between the Jansenists and *le siècle des lumières*. Three areas are suggested here for examination: some trends in Jansenism which had social and political implications; the religious basis of the Jansenist ideology; and possible links between Jansenists and the advanced guard of the Enlightenment in France.[2]

I

Religious history in France in the eighteenth century has been largely written, as the historian Dominique Julia pointed out recently, either from a literary aspect, following the tradition of Sainte-Beuve and Henri Bremond, or as a chapter in the history of Church and state. This is particularly true with eighteenth-century Jansenism where the entire emphasis has tended to be given to the Jansenist-Gallican and *richériste* conflicts with the Church hierarchy and the monarchy. Therefore, Julia suggested that the development of Jansenism as a social phenomenon has still to be examined in depth,[3] — for example, in studies at the level as that of René Taveneaux on Jansenism in the province of Lorraine.[4] While we wait for such monographs we can attempt to sketch some broad lines of the development that occurred in Jansenism as it adjusted to the new circumstances that followed its condemnation in the papal bull *Unigenitus* in 1713. The development, it seems fair to say, was mainly a reorientation; many of the basic insights remained, yet it led to that new phenomenon known as the "second" Jansenism.

Jansenism grew originally from a theological debate about the nature of man and his relationship with God; it flourished between two revolutions, the Reformation and the French Revolution, at a time when absolutism and the centralized state were being consolidated. The debate was touched off because of dissatisfaction with the efforts of the counter-Reform movement to adjust its theology to the new outlook and ideals of Renaissance humanism. Hence the lengthy discussions on the nature of man, human liberty, original sin and grace. Manifestations of the dissatisfaction took various forms. French Jansenism followed two main lines of development in the seventeenth century.[5] One tended to reject the world and secular life, a position adopted by the founder, Jansenius, and two of his early stalwarts — his friend, the abbé de Saint-Cyran, Jean Duvergier de Hauranne (1581–1643), and Martin de Barcos (1600–1678), one of the spiritual directors of Port-Royal. Another group, while sharing the first's deep uneasiness with the world, gradually adopted a more moderate position which allowed greater involvement in secular life and concern with contemporary political and social problems. For them the world was worth saving and human earthly happiness a good to be sought. Antoine Arnauld (1612–1694) and Pascal (1623–1662) adopted this stance, which, in the long run, probably had the most influence among later Jansenists.

It is the latter, more moderate strand of Jansenism we shall now examine in some detail.

Pierre Nicole (1625–1695) belonged to this moderate school and in his *Essais de Morale* (1671–1678) provided an important Jansenist position statement which had considerable influence through the eighteenth century. His ideas on political and social life were sketched out in one part of his *Essais*, the "Traité de l'éducation d'un prince." Society and the state, he pointed out, are necessities, happy inventions, to preserve peace and order and provide the needs of the populace. Social utility is the basis of state and government; reason is the guiding light which can direct a state to perform its functions in a very imperfect world, an instrument which God uses to direct man to good works. Each component of the state has responsibilities and duties to seek peace and order — notably the monarch, who has a providential role in society, but also the individual citizen, who has responsibilities as a member of the human family "since the whole world is our city."[6]

For the moderates as well as the strict Jansenists, however, individual salvation was the all important aim of life, and this was to be accomplished whether one belonged to a group, a caste or an institution. Thus Jansenism represented a tension between a sturdy individualism in the essentials of human living and a hierarchical society, a society of orders where aims and ideals were to be inspired and regulated according to one's order. Thus the Jansenist represented a kind of gadfly, always at least an implicit critic of the contemporary scene. Saint-Simon spoke of the problem that Louis XIV saw in them, "having been raised by the queen his mother in the firm conviction that those who were called Jansenists formed a republican party within the church and state and were sworn enemies of his absolute rule which was the idol he worshipped."[7] But as René Taveneaux has noted, while Jansenists may have been regarded by the Court as dangerous, they were revolutionary only in the spiritual order, adding a ferment to society through their spiritual ideals and their stress on individual responsibility and the role of conscience. And thus there appeared, in time, an inherent paradox in Jansenism. Though born out of a reaction to humanism and the Renaissance, it eventually adopted some of the ideals of humanism by stressing the autonomy of the individual conscience, "assisting if not in the origins, at least in the development, of the liberal spirit."[8]

Nicole belonged to the first generation of Jansenists and died towards the end of the seventeenth century. A friend of his, Jacques Duguet (1649–1733), was one of the chief links with the second generation and continued the Jansenists' interest in social and political ideas. He was primarily a religious writer, one of the best of the eighteenth century, a moralist and educator who was highly regarded by his contemporaries. Voltaire is said to have regarded him as the best of the Jansenist writers, and his many works went through several editions.[9] The one work which had the greatest success was his *Institution d'un prince*, written in 1699 and published in 1739, intended as a guide for the heir to the throne of Piedmont.[10]

Duguet's aim in this work was to describe an ideal Christian state, and the ideal Christian prince to govern it, and to point out the errors and deficiencies to be avoided. In his criticism of contemporary government he echoed the sentiments of La Bruyère and Fénelon, though, as Sainte-Beuve remarked, he did not have the literary abilities to compose a *Télémaque*.[11] Of the four sections in the work, one is given over to the education of a prince, two to relations between Church and state, and one to the duties of a prince. The core of Duguet's advice is that the ultimate duty of the governor is to look to the happiness of his people; and this is to be done by giving more attention to agriculture, lowering taxes, economizing in the use of public funds and administering justice fairly.[12] Some of his recommendations are radical enough —the curtailing of the sale of magistrates, offices, the disbanding of the system of tax farming. However, the most novel aspect of his discourse is the emphasis, resembling that of the later physiocrats and agronomists, which he gives to economic life. The moralist appears even in this section, in his pointing to the dangers of too great stress being placed on manufacturing, which in time would take away the livelihood of the small artisan and increase the influence of the monied class in the state.[13] The work was condemned by the prime minister, Cardinal Fleury, not because of Duguet's economic ideas, but because, as D'Argenson has suggested, he warned of the dangers of a king giving too much power to a prime minister.[14] It was also condemned by the Church, possibly because he seemed to recommend the election of bishops.

Duguet's *Institution* was written before the promulgation of *Unigenitus* and thus before the intimate alliance of Jansenists with the *parlementaires*. Condemnation by Church and state was to instill gradually a greater political aggressiveness into the party as it joined the critical ferment of the Regency period. Jansenists were to be found who were not content to lecture the king on his duties but were ready to question the very source of the monarch's authority. One of these, a Jansenist priest of considerable prominence at the time, Nicolas Le Gros (1675-1751), pointed out that the experience of the king's enforced accepting of the papal bull could teach many lessons. Was it not essential, he asked, to remember that God bestows on states the right to govern its people? "This authority is more essentially attached to Society than to the leaders who govern it. The persons who exercise authority die and are replaced by others; the body does not die." This, he said, is obvious when the government is elected, but also seems true in monarchies even where the monarchy is hereditary and absolute, for "kings are always ministers of God and the Republic."[15] As it became clear that the parlement was the only institution left to support them, the Jansenists expounded again and again the traditional thesis of the parlement as the depositary and interpreter of fundamental law.

By mid-century a more complete statement of Jansenist political thought was possible. The spokesman was Pierre Barral (?-1772) who in 1754 published two works: *Maximes sur le devoir des rois* and *Manuel des souverains*. The first book was a collection of counsels for a monarch gathered from sermons, moral books and philosophers, and from a wide variety of writers, including Erasmus, Fénelon, Bossuet, the ancient philosophers and Duguet. The second work is more original and attracted considerable attention shortly after publication, prompting a new edition in London in 1755, under the title *Principes sur le gouvernement*. The influence of Duguet is apparent in Barral's comments on the purpose and necessity of government and civil society, for "the happiness of a nation, such is the purpose of legislation in every state."[16] And again: "The duty of a prince is

30

nothing else to conform to the laws, and to oblige others to conform, to look to the happiness of the people, and interest himself
in the welfare of the Nation and of individuals...to favour the
progress of virtue and to reward it." On economic matters he
wrote: "The cultivation of the land and industry are the basis of
all wealth and consequently the two areas that the business of
finance should consider...It is commerce and shipping which
bring wealth to the individual and to the state, and which render
the Prince more powerful, more respected, and more feared by his
neighbours."[17]

But a guarantee is necessary that the monarch fulfil his obligations; a watchdog is necessary to protect the state against arbitrary
government and absolutism. "Far from regarding registration of
laws as an empty ceremony," he noted, "sovereigns are obliged to
accept it as a basic formality of State, inseparable from the legitimate use of legislation; it ensures that monarchs provide good
laws for their people; and the people in turn are ensured that they
are well governed by kings."[18] His statements are not unlike the
Remonstrances of the Parlement de Paris in the 1750s and 1760s,
and his defence of parlement as a vital force in government echoes
Montesquieu's *Esprit des lois*. The parlement is essential because
its function is to safeguard the throne, to conserve authority and
to ensure that laws are observed, on which rest domestic peace
and the safety and security of the prince.[19]

One of the chief responsibilities of the monarch, according to
Barral, is the welfare of the Church and the careful direction of
relations between Church and state. He is to protect the Church
from external and internal enemies, and therefore must protect it
from the despotism of the bishops, who also are called to be
ministers and dedicated to the common good, "un ministère et
non pas un Empire." Above all the monarch must distinguish
between rights of the clergy and abuses, between freedom in
administering sacraments and exorbitant claims of independence
made by the bishops.[20]

Barral was succeeded as spokesman for the political wing of the
Jansenist party by a highly vocal member of the Parlement de
Paris and canon lawyer, Gabriel Maultrot (1714–1803). He published over forty books, most of them dealing with the relationship of Church and state, but on occasion he launched into
discourses on the monarchy, for example in *Origine et étendue
de la puissance temporelle* (1789–1791), which appeared towards

the end of his writing career. Maultrot was influenced by Le Gros and by Barral, first in that he insisted that all power of government is based in the nation and is delegated to the ruler, and second in his belief that the monarchy must be controlled by various checks and balances, like the parlement. However, he broke new ground in his unqualified rejection of the divine right of kings, sponsoring a purely utilitarian theory of the origins of monarchy. The authority of a monarch comes from God; the power of a monarch cannot be compared, for instance, with that of a bishop — the latter's power comes from a sacrament, and there is nothing sacramental about the crowning of a king. The power of a king is bestowed upon him by the people, and thus his power comes from a basic liberty in man, which, in turn, is a gift of God. Why then, said Maultrot, look to heaven for a power based on human liberty, why multiply miracles without necessity?[21] His theory of government seems to consist of a constitutional monarchy: "To the nation God confers legislative power; to a king is given an entirely different power, the power of execution."[22]

But in Maultrot's writings the political element is subordinated to his discussions on the role of the lower clergy in the French Church. He was the lower clergy's most vocal advocate in the second half of the eighteenth century. He was also an ardent Gallican, convinced that the monarchy had failed to uphold the Gallican tradition in its treatment of the Jansenists and in its subservient attitude to the pope and the bishops. Yet, in a sense, all his interests were tied up in the politics associated with the union of Church and state. On the one hand he argued that the monarchy should have more control over the Church; conversely he argued that all power over Church and state resides in the people and that kings are simply delegates of the people. And, with a certain consistency, when the civil constitution was promulgated in 1790, he found that this solution was not acceptable because it did not represent the will of the people and put the control of the Church completely in the hands of the secular powers.[23]

It is interesting to note that Maultrot had little to say about economic and social problems in contemporary France. His leading theme was a kind of rationalization or desacralization of royal power, to the benefit of the nation. In this he reflected a view on Jansenism described in 1772 by a representative of the Parlement de Paris: "With the suppression of the Jesuits in

France Jansenism lost much of its value and its driving force and was transformed into a party of *patriotisme*. One must give credit for it always was greatly attracted to an independent approach: with invincible courage it fought against the despotism of the popes; but political despotism is a hydra no less dangerous and it should now direct its forces towards this present enemy since they are no longer needed for the other combat."[24] Yet for Maultrot there were restrictions to be placed on the transfer of power to the nation for, as noted above, he insisted on a clear distinction being made between the temporal and the spiritual. Nor was he necessarily advocating democracy, despite his championing of a government devoid of all the trappings of religious symbols, such as rule by divine right. In fact, a friend of Maultrot, Grégoire Herluison, thought that this was one of the weaknesses among the heirs to the Port-Royal tradition, that they had not gone far enough in their defence of the rights of the lower clergy or in arguing for the rights of the nation: "They had indeed brought to light the rights of the temporal authority with reference to the spiritual powers, but the time had still not come to demonstrate the rights of the nations."[25] However, it is remarkable how far the Jansenists moved — from the position of Nicole to that of Maultrot on the eve of the Revolution — grappling with ideas which moved steadily towards a greater participation in government, possibly a form of democracy, and certainly at least a form of constitutional monarchy.

II

Important questions are raised by the increasingly radical political thought of the Jansensists: What was the motivation behind it? How convinced were they of their incipient liberal ideas? There is not doubt that some of their inspiration came from their long history of opposition; they sought change from a desire for their own survival and, in some instances, exemplified by their alliance with the parlement, from pragmatism so as to ensure some change in the political and ecclesiastical system. But to say that self-protection was their sole inspiration implies that the Jansenism of the eighteenth century was devoid of any organized and coherent doctrine and was simply a collection of disgruntled elements inside the Church. There is reason to see in the "second" Jansenism a different and more developed form of the religious insights of the founders.

In his *European Thought in the Eighteenth Century*, Paul Hazard spoke of what he called "enlightened Christianity"; he described it as "a movement, European in scope, and aiming at freeing religion from the accretion which had accumulated about it, and at presenting a creed so liberal in doctrine that no one in the future could accuse it of obscurantism, so transparently clear in its moral teaching that no one henceforth could deny its practical efficiency."[26] Hazard was inclined to think that this phenomenon was to be found outside France, but, as Bernard Plongeron has recently observed, there were traces of it in France too, particularly after 1750 among the Jansensists. This can be illustrated by a brief look at the Jansenist discussion on the nature of the Church and on what reforms were necessary in it. This kind of discussion was to be the source of so many of their political ideas.

In examining Barral's theory on the relationship between the monarch and the Church, we noted that he emphasized the role of the king in controlling bishops who were inclined to act like absolute monarchs. He argued that the institutional church is not an empire to be ruled by a despot, but a ministry, whose chief function is to minister to the interior religious needs of the people. This idea was taken up in the Jansenist paper *Les Nouvelles ecclésiastiques* after 1750; for the next forty years it was given prominence in the paper and, as a result, wide-spread attention. In a theme that goes back to the early Jansenists, the paper again and again stressed a distinction between the Church as an institution or a political entity, and the church as an assembly of the faithful dedicated to the deepening of the religious life of the community. The evils they saw in the Church came from too great an emphasis on externals, — for example, the power of the bishops — and from modifying its doctrines to make them more palatable to the contemporary world. What was needed to counteract these evils were a greater study and use of the scriptures and a reformed liturgy, in the vernacular, which would afford a greater participation of the faithful. One of the main reasons, said the Jansenist paper, why the piety of the people is so superficial is that they do not understand what is being said in the liturgy or what is being signified by the actions of the liturgy.[27]

The aim was clear enough. What this Jansenist writer wanted, as did his contemporaries and predecessors, was a revitalizing of Christianity, progress in the deepening of religious life by a return to the spirit and customs of the early church. Thus they insisted that they were not sponsoring a new theology or a new morality but were simply restating the doctrines and moral teachings of the initial church as interpreted by the great teacher Augustine. The so-called Jansenists were simply followers of St. Augustine; Jansenism, as a system of doctrines to be condemned, was simply a construct of the enemies of the truth. They were not heretics, they were not Calvinists, they accepted the essentials of the Church and its sacraments, but they believed in a Church always desirous of reformation.

To bring about reformation, however — and this was the crucial point — a modification had to take place in the pyramid structure of the Church, and power, which the Jansenists usually interpreted as meaning secular power, had to be removed from the Church authorities. Thus excommunication ought to disappear. How much of the pyramid ought to remain? The *Nouvelles ecclé-siastiques*, in accord with Maultrot, was reluctant to have the laity share in the direction of the Church and was content to see only the lower clergy given a share, so that the Church would continue a form of aristocracy, with the "orders" of society still remaining.[28] This prompted critics, such as Herluison, to complain that the Jansenists were not daring enough even in their promoting the rights of the lower clergy. In February 1789, a curé from Châlons, reflecting on the increased political prominence of the lower clergy, asked who was responsible for the improvement. Obviously the Jansenists, he thought. But he noted that it was also partly the work of *philosophes*, such as Rousseau, Le Tourner and Mercier, in singing the praises of the humble curé. And he continued: "It must be stated that the theologians are sometimes very unjust in the attacks they make on the *philosophes* because theologians are not exempt from making foolish statements, and are unwilling to see any merit in those they consider enemies of religion." Then he listed some of the great men whose works he admired, among them Arnauld, Nicole, Pascal, Montesquieu, Locke, Rousseau, Condillac, Fontenelle and Helvétius.[29] Thus, "enlightened Christianity" for this curé could come from a variety of sources and be brought about in part by the joint efforts of the *philosophes* and the Jansenists.

III

This linking of Jansenists with *philosophes* to form a list of the great men who had influence on changes in society raises one last question to be discussed: the relationship between the Jansenists and the advanced guard of the French Enlightenment. Even a brief examination of the political and social thinking of some of the prominent Jansenists seems to indicate that there was more than a little in common between them and the early *philosophe* movement. (It is probably well to specify the "early" *philosophe* movement, or the early Enlightenment, up to 1750, though, as has been noted, there were overtones in some of the Jansenists' social and economic thought which resembled the physiocrats' doctrine.)

Since the aims of the Jansenists and the early *philosophes* were similar, up to a point, it is sometimes wondered why the two groups did not form a closer alliance in the 1730s and 1740s. But, as it has also been remarked, there were Jansenists and Jansenists, and the Jansenists who were wrapped up in the miracles and convulsion scenes of Paris in the 1730s made little appeal to the *philosophes* or, in fact, to the government. The widely publicized *Nouvelles ecclésiastiques*, by giving such prominence to these episodes, probably in the long run seriously hurt the Jansenists' cause before Enlightened opinion. René Pomeau, the authority on Voltaire's religion, has suggested that Voltaire's Deism was at least in its early stages a form of anti-Jansenism.[30]

And yet, as Barbier and other contemporary journalists indicated, Jansenism had immense support in Paris from a wide variety of social levels from the 1720s to the 1750s. The excitement over the revivalism and the enthusiasm associated with the miracles and the so-called convulsions accounts for part of it; sympathy for a persecuted group supported by the parlement, which was recognized as the last defender of freedom, explains more. To what extent the members of the parlement had Jansenist leanings, as opposed to Gallican aims, is still a question not easily answered, partly because Jansenism was not a systematic set of doctrines but more an attitude. Even some of those who accepted the condemnation of Jansenism in *Unigenitus* as necessary for the unity of the French Church still found it possible to have deep sympathy with the Jansenists' uneasiness and disquietude with weaknesses in the Church and with the worldliness of contemporary society. The Chancellor Daguesseau (1668–1751) seems to have been of this type. He was a man deeply upset over the treatment of the Port-Royal Jansenists by Louis XIV and a devoted disciple of the early Jansenists writers; at the same time he was alert to the need for change in society, particularly in the area of his responsibility as chancellor — the reform and codification of law.[31]

Similarly another group of Jansenist sympathizers, whom Emile Appolis has called the "third party" or para-Jansenists, and who were found largely among the clergy, meditated deeply about the need for reform in the Church. As Appolis pointed out, para-Jansenism was a European phenomenon which had support in the Roman Curia, but also had a following in Germany and Spain.[32] In Italy Jansenist interests would extend beyond reform of the Church to political and social ideals of the *Risorgimento*.[33] And it was known that Leopold of Tuscany was a subscriber to the *Nouvelles ecclésiastiques*. In France the situation was particularly complicated because that semi-offical Jansenist paper was consistently critical of the *philosophes*. Yet para-Jansenists among the French bishops, such as Fitz-James of Soissons, once the royal chaplain, and Montazet of Lyons, primate of France, maintained always a deep sympathy for Jansenism. Possibly because of this they showed an unusual interest in extending tolerance to the protestants and were alert to the fact that a cultural shift was taking place which required a changed attitude in the Church and a dialogue with the *philosophes* as leaders of opinion.[34] Both these bishops insisted on the need for the French Church to take a much more tolerant position towards the Jansenists. But after the mid-1760s, partly because of suppression of the Jesuits, the French hierarchy was exceedingly reluctant to conduct a dialogue either with the Jansenists or the *philosophes*.

And yet this is not to say that there was little or no influence from Jansenism on the *philosophes*. Robert Shackleton has noted that the spirit of opposition and criticism might account for some of the early philosophic inspiration of writers such as Fréret and the Encyclopedist Dumarsais, coming as they did from Jansenist schools.[35] And if Abbé Claude Goujet was not highly exceptional, Jansenists did take their places in the provincial academies and attained relatively high positions among the literary elite. Goujet, besides being entirely acceptable to the stern editors of the *Nouvelles ecclésiastiques* and an historian of the early Jansenists, can be acclaimed as a distinguished historian of French literature and the highly competent editor of Moréri's *Dictionnaire*. He compiled a library of over ten thousand volumes and an annotated catalogue of his books in which he has noted various compliments of Jesuits and *philosophes*.[36] Literary and history specialists among the Benedictines in Paris also seem to have had considerable sympathy for the Jansenist cause.[37] Other examples no doubt could be given. But in the long run it seems that the Jansenists' influence on the Enlightenment was derived from a desire for reform based on their religious and ecclestiastical ideology; thus their influence towards change and reform was a movement collateral to that of the philosophes. It is also true that, at times, some of the Jansenists' political aims might have been more radical than those of the *philosophes*, but always their range of interest and influence was to remain less cohesive and pointed.

C.B. O'Keefe, S.J.

Notes

1. Daniel Roche, "Encyclopédistes et académiciens: Essai sur la diffusion sociale des Lumières," in *Livre et société dans la France du XVIIIe siècle*, 2 vols. (Paris, 1965, 1970).

2. Of particular use is R. Taveneaux, *Jansénisme et politique* (Paris, 1965), a gathering of some excerpts from the Jansenists' writings, but most valuable for Taveneaux's comments; see also his recent *La Vie quotidienne des Jansénistes* (Paris, 1973). For some early explorations of the Jansenist-Enlightenment relationship, see R. Shackleton, "Jansenism and the Enlightenment," *Studies on Votaire and the Eighteenth Century* 57 (1967): 1387-97. For a comment on Shackleton's approach, see R. Darnton, "In Search of the Enlightenment: Recent Attempts to Create a Social History of Ideas," *Journal of Modern History*, March 1971, pp. 116-17. On the academies, see Roche, "Encyclopédistes et académiciens."

3. Dominique Julia, "Problèmes d'historiographie religieuse," *Dix-Huitième Siècle*, no. 5 (1973), pp. 81, 86. See also Louis Trénard, "Lumières et Révolution," *Dix-Huitième Siecle*, no. 6 (1974), pp. 26-27.

4. R. Taveneaux, *Le Jansénisme en Lorraine, 1640-1789* (Paris, 1960).

5. On the early splintering of Jansenism, see A. Adam, *Du Mysticisme à la révolte, Les Jansénistes du XVIIIe siècle* (Paris, 1968); Taveneaux, *La Vie quotidienne*, chap. 1-4; and J. Armogathe, "Jansénisme," in *Dictionnaire de spiritualité*, fasc. 52-53 (Paris, 1972).

6. On Nicole, see *Dictionnaire de théologie catholique*, s.v. "Nicole"; L. Rothkrug, *Opposition to Louis XIV: The Political and Social Origins of the French Enlightenment* (Princeton, 1965), pp. 50-55, 84-85; and Taveneaux, *Jansénisme et politique*, pp. 92-99, 237-38.

7. Saint-Simon, *Mémoires*, ed. L. Norton, 2 vols. (London, 1968), 2: 301.

8. R. Taveneaux, "Jansénisme et la vie sociale," *Revue d'histoire de l'église de France* 54 (1968): 46.

9. On Duguet, see Taveneaux, *Jansénisme et politique*, pp. 28-29, 100-112, 231-33; B. Plongeron, *Théologie et politique* (Paris, 1973), pp. 102-108; and Charles Augustin Sainte-Beuve, *Port-Royal, le cours de Lausanne* (Paris, 1937), pp. 540-78.

10. J. Duguet, *Institution d'un prince*, 4 vols. (Leyden, 1738).

11. Sainte-Beuve, *Port Royale*, p. 571.

12. Duguet, *Institution* 2: 249-53, 258-63.

13. *Ibid.*, pp. 282-89.

14. Marquis D'Argenson, *Mémoires et journal inédit*, 4 vols. (Paris, 1857-58), 2:165-66.

15. Nicolas Le Gros, *Du Renversement des libertés de l'église,* 2 vols (n.p., 1716), 1:344-45.

16. Pierre Barral, *Manuel des souverains* (n.p., 1754), pp. 28-29. See also Taveneaux, *Jansénisme et politique*, pp. 203-205, 229; and Plongeron, *Théologie et politique*, pp. 102-108.

17. Barral, *Manuel*, p. 14.

18. *Ibid.*, p. 171.

18. *Ibid.*, p. 160.

20. *Ibid.*, p. 203.

21. Gabriel Maultrot, *Origine et étendue de la puissance temporelle,* 3 vols. (Paris, 1789-90), 1:7-10. On Maultrot, see J. Carreyre, *Dictionnaire de Théologie catholique*, s.v. "Maultrot"; and E. Préclin, *Les Jansénistes du XVIIIe siècle* (Paris, 1929).

22. Maultrot, *La puissance temporelle* 1:19-20.

23. M. Picot, *Memoires pour servir à l'histoire ecclésiastique,* 4 vols. (Paris, 1816), 4:604-606; and Taveneaux, *Jansénisme et politique*, p. 216.

24. Mouffle D'Angerville, *Journal historique de la révolution opérée dans la constitution de la monarchie française*, 7 vols. (London, 1774), 2:351. (Michaud's *Biographie universelle* gives Amsterdam as the place of publication.) The author of the journal was a contributor to Bachaumont's *Mémoires secrets*.

25. G. Herlusion, *La Théologie réconciliée avec le patriotisme* (Troyes, 1790), p. 47.

26. Paul Hazard, *European Thought in the Eighteenth Century* (London, 1954), pp. 86-87.

27. *Nouvelles ecclésiastiques*, 1793, pp. 2-3; 1772, p. 186; 1778, p. 2. See also Bernard Plongeron, "Une Image de l'église d'après les 'Nouvelles Ecclésiastiques,' " *Revue d'histoire de l'église de France*, no. 151 (1976), pp. 252-58.

28. *Nouvelles ecclésiastiques*, 1778, p. 98; 1784, p. 50. See also Plongeron, "Une image de l'église," pp. 245-52.

29. Letter of a curé to the abbé de Grégoire, quoted in Taveneaux, *Le Jansénisme en Lorraine*, pp. 708-709.

30. R. Pomeau, *La Religion de Voltaire* (Paris, 1956), p. 27.

31. See Georges Frêche, *Un Chancelier gallican: Daguesseau* (Paris, 1969), pp. 38-42.

32. Emile Appolis, *Entre Jansénistes et zelanti: Le tiers-parti catholique au XVIIIe siècle* (Paris, 1960), pp. 217-47.

33. Maurice Vaussard, *Jansénisme et gallicanisme aux origines religieuses de Risorgimento* (Paris, 1959), pp. 13-45.

34. Appolis, *Entre Jansénistes et zelanti*, pp. 240-47.

35. Shackleton, "Jansenism and the Enlightenment," pp. 1391-93.

36. On Goujet, see Picot, *Mémoires* 4: 320-22; and *Biographie* universelle, s.v. "Goujet." Goujet's catalogue of books, still unpublished, is in the Bibliothèque Nationale (Paris), N.A.F. 1009-1013; it consists of a set of five volumes in which an elaborate system of book classification is worked out. For some comments about the library, see A. Tougard, *Catalogue de l'Abbé Goujet* (Paris, 1918).

37. Taveaux, *Le Jansénisme en Lorraine*, 659-63.

The Role of the Church in New France

When we speak of the Church in the eighteenth century, it has to be borne in mind that it consisted not merely of the clergy but of the laity as well. Moreover, the members of the Church, clergy and laity alike, had a dual obligation: to God and to their king. Their obligation to God was so to live in this world that they would be admitted, as belatedly as possible, to the kingdom of heaven. To achieve this end, in the Roman Church, the aid of the clergy was essential. This was their prime, but by no means only, function. The clergy's duty to the king was summed up in the oath of office of Monseigneur Pontbriand, bishop of Quebec, in 1741:

> I promise His Majesty that for as long as I live I will
> be his faithful subject and servant, that I will strive
> with all my strength to serve and to further the well
> being of his state; that I will not take part in any
> council, plot, or enterprise that could endanger it,
> and should anything untoward come to my attention,
> I will make it known to His Majesty, so help me God,
> and I so swear on his Holy Gospel.[1]

In New France, from the outset of the colony, there was a close alliance between the clergy and the Crown to further their common aims. It was, in fact, the Crown that initiated the work of the clergy in the area. In October 1604, Henri IV, through the agency of a Jesuit, Father Pierre Coton, asked Pope Aquaviva to provide two missionaries to accompany the French fishing fleet to the Grand Banks.[2] In that same year the French established a permanent base in the Bay of Fundy, but it was not until 1610 that a missionary was sent out and the first Indians rather summarily baptised.[3] This marked the beginning of a massive drive by Church and Crown to convert all the pagan nations of the continent to Christianity, and it proved to be a far more difficult task than had been imagined. The high hopes of the early Jesuits were not to be fulfilled.

There were several reasons for this lack of success, which cannot be gone into here. Suffice it to say that the economic base of the first French settlements in Acadia and on the banks of the

St. Lawrence was the trade in furs. The Indians were eager to give up their furs in exchange for European manufactured goods but very loath to entrust their souls to the Church of Rome. The French Crown, however, insisted that missionaries had to accompany the fur traders; hence the Indians had to tolerate the obnoxious black robes in their midst.

The capture of the French bases by an Anglo-Scots freebooting expedition in 1628-29, and the savage onslaughts of the Iroquois confederacy caused the Crown, the fur trade company and the missionaries to realize that there could be no hope of any of them achieving their aims unless more secure bases were established, bases which would be able to provide for their own basic material needs rather than depend on food and other supplies brought from France each summer. At this particular time the Crown could provide little aid, being embroiled in the Thirty Years' War. The fur trade company lacked the capital needed to establish settlers. It was, therefore, the Church, and more specifically, the Society of Jesus, that had to serve as an immigration agency.

The Jesuits succeeded in obtaining sizable sums of money from wealthy and devout individuals in France, as well as from a powerful secret society, the Compagnie de Saint-Sacrement, which might be described as resembling a blend of the present day Salvation Army, the Carnegie Foundation and the Mafia. (It was, for example, members of that Compagnie who provided the organization and finances for the establishment of a mission settlement at Montréal.⁴) The Jesuits also brought out labourers to clear land on the seigneuries granted them by the Crown, ready for settlers to put to the plough upon their arrival. Their stated purpose now became, to establish "A New Jerusalem, blessed by God and made up of citizens destined for heaven."⁵ Without this concerted effort by the Church, it is doubtful if New France would have survived until the restoration of peace and stability in France allowed Louis XIV to take the colonies out of the hands of the private companies in 1663 and make them wards of the Crown.

As the number of settlers increased, the role of the clergy became less that of a mission to the Indians and more of a mission to the French colonists. It had been hoped that the establishment of schools and a hospital to care for the Indians would induce them to embrace Christianity. The Indians spurned both. Even when a few Indian families were persuaded to send their children to the schools at Montréal and Québec, it proved impossible to keep them there. These wild creatures of the forest would not submit to the unaccustomed and harsh discipline. They fled back to their families at the first opportunity. Similarly, they preferred their own medicaments and the ministrations of their shamans to those of the French. (In this they displayed wisdom since only the strong and healthy could withstand the nostrums of current European medical practice.)

But once these institutions had been established, they were maintained to serve the settlers. Although by 1640 the population of New France was made up of only sixty-four families, and comprised 356 individuals — 158 men, 116 women including the religious, 29 Jesuits and 53 soldiers[6] — yet they had a school, a hospital and a college for advanced studies. Sizable towns in France might have envied them, particularly since they paid little or nothing for these institutions. It is a rather cruel irony that the Church, in establishing these firm foundations for European culture and civilization as a means to serve and save the Indians, thereby laid the groundwork for their eventual destruction.

From the outset, a main concern of the Church was to forfend in New France the appalling religious condition that existed in seventeenth-century France where the mass of the peasantry was more pagan than Christian and most of the rural parish priests were in little better case. Not only was the Church in France faced with the challenge of extirpating Calvin's heresy; it found itself faced with the greater and more urgent task of Christianizing the French people, and this required an educated clergy. In 1637 Father Beurrier, on arriving at his parish of Nanterre, declared that the villagers were ignorant of "those most common things that one must absolutely understand in order to receive the sacraments and be saved."[7] A bishop of Autun in the second half of the century informed the pope that in his diocese the people were "coarse, barely initiated into the primary principles of the faith, living in a dense and inveterate ignorance."[8] At the same time Father Julien Mannoir wrote that in lower Brittany the people knew so little of the Christian religion that his first task was to establish the rudiments of the faith.[9] Nor were many of the clergy much better. There were continual complaints of their drunkenness and bad morals. Few of them wore clerical garb and they were indistinguishable from the peasants. Non-residence in their parishes was all too frequent; some were seen there only once or twice a year. Many could not understand a word of Latin; they could stumble through the mass but had little understanding of its meaning.[10] The only instruction the vast majority had received was a few lessons from a local curé, either a relative or a close neighbour.[11] This condition had existed for a long time. It was the religious revival, engendered by the Reformation, that threw it into stark relief and, perhaps, exaggerated it. The lingering stirrings of the old rural paganism, which sanctified a spring, an ancient tree or a wishing stone and required the excommunication of annoying wasps, now was regarded askance by the learned doctors at the Sorbonne.[12] So too was the burning of witches.[13]

In New France from the outset the religious climate was placed on a much higher plane. The clergy who came to the colony were nearly all exceptionally well educated, and highly motivated. This was particularly true of the Jesuits and the Sulpicians, but the secular clergy also were hand-picked by the directors of the *Missions Etrangères* in Paris. The members of the women's orders, the Ursulines, Hôpitalières and the Congrégation de Notre Dame, were drawn from the educated class, and one has only to read the letter of Marie de l'Incarnation to become aware of the extreme fervour that possessed them.[14] Moreover, in New France no purely contemplative orders were permitted; the clergy all had to perform useful social functions.

After the assumption of royal control in 1663, although Church and state worked in close harmony, there was never any question that the Crown was the dominant partner. The bishop was nominated by the king and 40 percent of the funds at the Church's disposal were sparingly doled out by the Crown.[15] The clergy were closely checked by the intendant and the Sovereign Council at every turn.[16] The Crown decided how many clergy there would be and defined their roles. To a considerable degree they were agents of the Crown. There were, it is true, a few spirited conflicts between clergy and royal officials in the seventeenth century, but these were more clashes of personality than conflicts over principle. Some historians, however, have made far too much of them, viewing the seventeenth century through latter-day orange-tinted spectacles. What is much more significant is the degree to which royal officials and senior clergy worked in harmony. The reason for this is that they were, after all, members of the same Church and were agreed on the premises that governed their society, premises so basic that they were unstated and taken for granted.

Nor can it be said — but of course it has — that the colony was priest ridden. In 1698, there were 308 clergy in Canada, 2.2 percent of the population. By 1712, their numbers had increased by four, but they now represented only 1.6 percent. At the end of the seventeenth century, there was one church per 223 souls, and in 1713 one per 246. In 1759, there were fewer than 200 clergymen to serve a population of some 75,000 to 80,000 people.[17] Canada under the French regime was far from being a theocracy. If one seeks a theocracy in America, one should look towards seventeenth-century Massachusetts, not Canada.

Indeed, during the period soon after 1663, when immigrants poured in, raising the population from 3,300 to some 11,000 in less than a decade, the problem was to find enough clergy to serve the people. The few there were were worked to death, travelling winter and summer by canoe and snowshoe throughout the settlements to say mass and administer the sacraments. This proved too much for some of the secular priests; one-third of the first group to arrive gave up after a year and returned to France.[18] As late as 1683 the intendant complained that at least three-quarters of the *habitants* did not hear mass more than four times a year.[19] It was to remedy this deplorable situation that Bishop Laval, immediately upon his arrival at Québec, had set about establishing a seminary. Its chief aim was to provide a native Canadian clergy, but boys who did not intend to enter the clergy were not excluded. Although the poorer students paid no fees, it cannot be claimed that this seminary enjoyed overwhelming success. The regulations, which were strictly enforced, perhaps explain why. The boys admitted had to be at least ten years old on entry, for the simple reason that few children younger than that had the manual dexterity needed to use a quill pen, which was the only writing instrument available. But at that age children were capable of performing chores on their parents' farms, and, given the desperate shortage of labour in the colony, few *habitant* families could forgo their children's services.

The boys admitted to the Seminary had to have no physical deformity and be of a devout disposition. They rose at 4:00 in the morning during the summer months, slept in till 4:30 in winter. They attended classes and devotions until 8:00 at night, then retired. They wore a distinctive uniform: a blue parka coat with a sash, and a wide-brimmed hat. Their hair was cut short, their meals provided the minimum of food, barely enough to maintain health, and they were permitted to bathe no oftener than was deemed absolutely necessary. Plays and all other amusements had to be shunned, and the young students had to see as little as possible of their own families, keep them at arm's length, to avoid an overly emotional attachment to the secular world.[20] It should, therefore, come as no surprise that of the first 200 students, 135 dropped out, most of them after one or two years. Despite this, or perhaps owing to a subsequent relaxation of this rigorous ascetic regime, the Québec seminary, over a ninety-year period took on 843 students, 118 of whom were eventually ordained.[21]

By 1760, of the seventy-three parish priests in the colony, four-fifths of them were Canadian born.[22] If Montcalm is to be believed (and on some few matters he can be) by the 1750s the curés were recruited from among the more well-to-do colonial families and, unlike their counterparts in France, were economically well off. He remarked in his journal that they were more respected than the clergy in France, and better housed. The average income of the curés was, he stated, 2,000 *livres* a year, and even the poorer parishes provided a stipend of 1,200, three times the wages of a Canadian artisan or a curé in France.[23] The Recollet order also attracted Canadians; in 1760 seventeen of the twenty-four were Canadian born. The Jesuits, however, only recruited three, and only one of them served in the colony.[24] It could be that more Canadians would have been accepted into the priesthood had it not been that the authorities, both clerical and secular, came to regard those who had entered with a rather jaundiced eye. The same complaint was made of them as of the laity. They were accused of being proud and independent, lacking in humility and not at all inclined to recognize, let alone submit to their superiors. It was for this reason that, in 1726, the Intendant Bégon counselled the bishop to have a dean for the cathedral sent from France rather than appoint a Canadian, and the bishop was in complete agreement.[25]

In the field of secular education, by the second quarter of the eighteenth century, the colony was quite well endowed. The Sulpicians had a school for boys at Montréal, and one of the main aims of the Hôpital there was to train schoolmasters to serve in the rural areas. It was the aim of both the royal officials and the clergy to have a school in every parish to teach the children "to pray, to read, and to write."[26] By the end of the regime about half the parishes had a school of sorts. In 1727, despite the fact that a lay school teacher's salary was only 375 *livres* a year, it became necessary to establish standards. In that year legislation was enacted requiring any would-be teachers to submit to an examination, obtain the sanction of the intendant and the bishop, then submit to the surveillance of the curé in the parish where he or she would teach. Male teachers could not teach girls, unless they were married, without special permission. The same regulation applied to single female teachers where the teaching of boys was concerned. Teachers were also required to set a good example to their students, avoiding taverns, games of chance, the company of those who lived too freely and persons of the opposite sex.[27]

The Ursulines had schools for girls at Quebéc and Trois Rivières, and the Sisters of the Congrégation de Notre Dame had schools in Montréal and in some of the outlying parishes. As well as mastering the regular curriculum the girls were expected to learn civility and the social graces, how to converse, how to please. Judging by the comments of the Swedish professor of botany, Peter Kalm, who visited the colony at mid-century, they were eminently successful.[28]

Despite the availability of these schools, few Canadians appear to have taken advantage of them. We have no reliable statistics on the literacy rate, but judging by the contracts in the notarial archives, a very small percentage of the *habitants* could read or write. Of a representative sample of seventy-five engagements of voyageurs in 1750, only two of those employed were able to sign their names.[29] Moreover, the presence of a signature is not proof of literacy. Some people learned to sign their name quite legibly but they could do no more than that; it was merely their mark. In any event, the vast majority of the *habitants* could live out their lives without any real need for literacy. There was at least one active merchant in Montréal who could not sign his name on a contract. If one member of a family was literate, that sufficed, and usually it was a female member who acquired the skill.

The curriculum, as well as the high standards, of the schools was likely also a factor. It comprised reading, writing, Latin, the catechism, civility, contracts and arithmetic. The schools were divided into eight grades: those learning the alphabet; those learning to spell; those learning to form syllables; those reading Latin phrases; those reading French; those learning to write; and those learning Latin grammar. No child was to move to a high grade until he had mastered the work of the lower group, and no student was to begin learning to read French until he was well versed in Latin.[30] It is difficult to see how a curriculum such as this could have had much utility, let alone appeal, for the some three-quarters of the population who spent their lives tilling the soil, paddling a canoe to the far west or voyaging on a schooner to Louisbourg.

The curing of bodies as well as of souls was also largely the responsibility of the Church. In Canada, however, this was never the problem that it was in France where the great mass of the people lived at the subsistence level most of the time and below it at recurring intervals. There, crop failures were frequent, causing the price of grain to soar; the people then starved to death by the thousands. (This was the reason why the population of France remained stable at nineteen to twenty million throughout the seventeenth and early eighteenth centuries — deaths equalled births.) In seventeenth-century France, unlike in England where the medieval system of private charity had collapsed and was replaced by a Poor Law — which was really a law against the poor — the Church launched a great program of social reform. St. Vincent de Paul was its leading protagonist. The aim was to awaken in the rich a sense of their obligation to aid the weaker members of society and thereby save their own souls.[31] *Bureaux de charité* and *hôpitaux généraux* were established by the Church, with bequests from individuals and some state or municipal aid, to care for the indigent, widows, orphans, cripples and the moribund. The Crown hoped to solve the terrible problem posed by hordes of vagabonds and diseased, starving poor by the establishment in every town of an *hôpital général* where the indigent could be housed (incarcerated might be the better term), given work to do and disciplined into leading useful and starkly moral Christian lives. The *bureaux de charité* were intended to assist people who required only temporary help to tide them over a crisis. Neither institution proved to be effective. The problem was far too great for these institutions, with their very limited resources, to resolve.[32]

In New France, poverty, and all the ills that accompany it, was never anything like the problem that it was in France. The abundance of arable land, absence of taxation and the flow of funds into the colony from the Crown and agencies of the Church effectively removed the spectre of starvation. It was generally accepted that a family had to care for its immediate members. Aged parents had to be provided for by their children. If a family failed in this obligation and it came to the attention of the intendant, he quickly issued an *ordonnance* obliging them to make the necessary provision for the indigent member.[33]

Yet there were still some few among the settlers who lacked this source of aid and were unable to provide for themselves: orphans, widows, some of the aged, cripples and others who had to resort to seeking alms. To cope with this problem the Church and the Crown merely introduced the institutions recently established in France, *hôpitaux généraux* and *bureaux des pauvres*. An *hôpital* was established in Montréal in 1688 by Jean-François Charon, a wealthy merchant, who founded the charitable and educational society, Les Frères hôpitaliers de Saint-Joseph de la Croix. The letters patent granted by the king in 1692 stated that the purpose of the community was "to take in poor orphan children, the crippled, the aged, the infirm, and other males in need, there to lodge, feed, and support them, put them to the work they are capable of doing, teach the said children a trade and give them the best education possible."[34] In 1747 the institution was taken over by a cloistered women's order, Les Soeurs Grises de la Charité, founded by Madame Youville.[35]

At Québec, Bishop Saint-Vallier established an *hôpital* on the outskirts of the town in 1692, over the strong opposition of the intendant, Jean Bochart de Champigny, who believed the funds could be put to better use in providing more curés for rural parishes.[36] Saint-Vallier spent 60,000 *livres* of his own funds on the institution and within a few years it was hard pressed to care for all who needed its assistance.[37] In 1707 it had forty inmates. In 1721 the Crown agreed to pay for a separate building to house the insane,[38] and by 1748 the Hôpital housed over eighty incurables and lunatics.[39]

These *hôpitaux* had a dual purpose: to assist the deserving poor, putting a stop to their importuning the rest of society, and to force the undeserving poor, the lazy who preferred begging, to honest toil, to finding gainful employment, of which there was rarely any shortage. In 1688, when the towns became flooded with mendicants as a result of an influenza epidemic that had left scores of families without breadwinners, Intendant Champigny had the Sovereign Council issue a *règlement* establishing *bureaux des pauvres* in the towns to provide assistance for the needy. They were staffed by the local curés and three lay directors, and depended on voluntary contributions for support. Once the crisis was over the *bureaux* ceased to function.[40]

It is not without significance that it was a royal official who took the initiative here. In fact, with all these institutions the Crown maintained a very tight control, auditing the accounts, providing much of their revenue, ruling on the expansion of facilities and the number of staff, which was always kept to a bare minimum.

This same crown control was exercised over the *hôtels Dieu*, which were hospitals as we understand the term today. The three towns had such hospitals when there were only an handful of settlers, at Québec in 1639, at Montréal in 1642, and at Trois Rivières in 1702. At the latter town it was again Bishop Saint-Vallier who took the initiative. When he became aware of the pressing need for a hospital he bought a house with his own funds, endowed it with 1,000 *livres* a year, and turned it over to the Ursulines to operate.[41] Here were treated those who could not be cured by their family physicians, but who were expected to recover. Those who could afford it were expected to pay, those who could not received treatment free.[42] The quality of the medical care would appear to have been high. During the Seven Years' War, when epidemics of typhus and smallpox, along with a large number of wounded, strained the *hôtels Dieu's* facilities to the limit, Montcalm reported that the troops could not have been better treated. In a dispatch to the minister he stated, "You will see, My Lord, by the attached troop return that the losses [from sickness] in the four battalions are far below what they would be in peace time in France."[43]

When these institutions were first established, the staffs were recruited in France by their respective mother houses, but it was not long before they came to be drawn from among the colonial families. In the *hôtels Dieu* and the *hôpitaux* there were three distinct social grades, performing different functions. At the top were the *religieuses de choeur* or chancel sister, below them the *converses* or lay sisters who took minor vows, and at the bottom the *données*. The *religieuses de choeur* were drawn from among the seigneurial families, and they had to bring with them a dowry of 3,500 *livres*. (Only a few of the very fashionable orders in France demanded a larger dowry than that, and most required much less.[44]) These sisters led a lady-like existence, only in times of urgency did they serve in the wards. The dirty work of caring for the sick was done by the *converses*, recruited from the artisan and *habitant* class, while the *données* performed the duties of domestic servants in return for their keep.[45] A few members of the lower social orders became *soeurs de choeur*, usually because well-to-do families sponsored them. It might be thought that only girls who could not find a husband entered the orders, but this is belied by the fact that the normal age on entry was nineteen. There were even some English girls, from the thirteen colonies, who entered the orders. These were girls who had been taken prisoner when children by Indians, ransomed by the French and cared for by the nuns. After conversion to the Roman faith, some of them found they had a vocation and were admitted to an order. In 1712 the governor and intendant reported that Marie Silver and Esther Owelin would not need the letters of naturalization granted by the king as the one had entered the Ursulines and the other the hôpitalières at Montréal.[46] Another such girl, Esther Wheelwright of Maine, a ward of the governor-general, entered the Ursulines and eventually became mother superior at Québec. It was she who greeted Wolfe's officers when they paid a courtesy call after the surrender of the city.

In addition to serving the King indirectly by caring for the physical needs of his decrepit subjects, some of the clergy served him directly as political and military agents. The missionaries with the Indians were required to keep them in the French alliance, to do everything possible to remove or reduce Anglo-American influence. Examples of this activity in the eighteenth century were afforded by the Jesuit, Father Sebastien Rasle, missionary to the Abenakis, who was killed by a New England raiding party in 1724 — several previous attempts to eliminate him had failed — and by the famous Abbé Le Loutre, missionary to the Micmacs on the border of Nova Scotia. Father Rasle exerted his considerable influence over the Abenakis to prevent New England encroachments on the Anglo-French borderlands. The Abbé Le Loutre also employed diplomacy and political maneuvering, but in addition he served as an active partisan military leader, and a highly skilled one.[47] The missionaries were required to keep the governor-general informed of all that transpired in their regions and pass on his orders and instructions to the military commanders of the western posts.[48] In short, they served as couriers and intelligence agents. Similarly, on the eve of war, some of them were sent on missions to the English colonies to discover all they could of the enemy's intentions and dispositions.[49] For this task Jesuits were employed since their order had papal sanction to wear civilian clothes when it would further the work of the church.

In a more peaceful vein the Church served to bind the colonial society firmly together. It was a highly status-ordered society, with a rigid hierarchical framework, modeled on that of France. It was at the church, every week, that these social gradations were made manifest. The ladies vied with each other to show off what they believed to be the latest court fashions, sometimes to the dismay of the curé looking down from his pulpit on rather startling décolletages. At mass social status was made evident by the position of the family pew — the closer to the altar the higher the status. To attempt to lease a pew farther forward than one's social position deemed fit was to create a scandal. The notarized contracts for the leasing of a pew are quite revealing. The exact position was stated, and once leased it could not be raised above the level of the other pews, nor any changes made to it that would incommode the other pew holders. A pew passed from generation to generation, in direct line, on payment of a 10 *livre* mutation fee, and it could not be transferred out of the line without the sanction of the church wardens. In the Montréal parish church the initial charge for a pew close to the altar was 75 *livres*, with an annual rent of 11 or 12 *livres*.[50] In the rural churches the rates were much lower, but the regulations were every bit as strict. The seigneur received the first pew by right; he and the members of his family received communion and all the other honors first; the curé had to offer a specific prayer for them by name; and when they departed this vale of tears they could be buried beneath their pew.[51] After the leading families had assumed their places, the rest of society squabbled over points of precedence, especially over the position they could occupy in religious processions, this despite strict rules laid down by the Sovereign Council.[52]

In addition to regulating social status, the churches themselves must have had a beneficial effect on the aesthetic sense of the Canadians. As the eighteenth century wore on, wooden churches were replaced with well-proportioned stone buildings. Unlike the bleak chapels of New England, in those of New France all the physical senses were catered to. The interiors were beautifully decorated with gilded woodcarving, the paneled walls painted cream with blue and silver trim. At mass the incense must have compensated for the reluctance of the people of that age to immerse themselves in water. The church bells governed the hours of labour in the fields, and in the towns the church organ offered the communality the pleasure of fine music. As early as 1661 the church at Québec had an organ and some years prior to 1721 a master organ builder was at work in Montréal.[53]

Finally, to examine briefly the religious climate of New France. it is virtually impossible to say exactly what their religion meant to the colonists. The vast majority were illiterate, and those of the laity who could write did not discuss religious matters. That the mass of the Canadians were well versed in the tenets of their faith there can be no doubt. Unity of religion in the colony precluded the violent disputes and debates that reveal so much about New England's religious climate. All that we can glean is an oblique view of the situation in the impressionistic comments by visitors, and the complaints of the clergy and royal officials about certain attitudes of the people. Thus we can deduce that until 1663 a distinctly puritanical attitude prevailed that has been mistaken by some for Jansenism. After that date, with the influx of immigrants come to seek their fortune, the climate became much more worldly. Montréal, for example, ceased to be merely a missionary base and became the commercial center for the fur trade and a military garrison town.

In the eighteenth century there were continual complaints at the way the people behaved at mass and in religious processions; being drunk and disorderly was the least of their sins. More significantly, there was a distinct decline in moral standards which mirrored that in contemporary France.[54] Proof of this is to be found in the rapid escalation in the number of foundlings, who were all made wards of the crown and who were all presumed to have been born out of wedlock. The intendant, who had to include an item in his budget for their upkeep, certainly regarded them as illegitimate since he labeled it *Enfants bâtards*. In 1736 it amounted to almost 14,000 *livres*: 1,042 for Trois Rivières, 4,970 for Québec, 7,956 for Montréal where the bulk of the regular troops were stationed.[55]

There is one revealing difference between France and New France regarding these rejected infants. In France many such children, some 40,000 a year were abandoned, left to die. Infanticide was a form of birth control.[56] In New France this phenomenon was unknown. The royal officials had little difficulty in finding families willing to take legal charge of the foundlings, including the occasional Indian baby, and assume responsibility for them until they reached the age of 18.[57] The reason for his difference in attitude is not hard to find. The rapid expansion of the population in mid-eighteenth-century France caused it to exceed the available food supply. Surplus children, legitimate as well as illegitimate, had to be abandoned; otherwise the entire family would have starved. There was no such problem in New France; instead, additional children were welcomed as a future source of labour.

Despite all these superficial indications of a lack of respect for the cloth and a somewhat less than devout attitude towards their religion, there is one piece of evidence to the contrary that is quite convincing. The eminent demographer Jacques Henripin, in his study of the eighteenth-century Canadian population, collated statistics on the dates of conception of children born in the country. When placed on a graph they show a steady line during the winter months, then a very sharp decline in April, followed by a sharp rise to a peak in July, then a decline to the level of the preceding winter months for the remainder of the year.[58] When one asks why there should have have been this marked aberration one is forced to the ineluctable conclusion that the sharp decline in the spring occurred because it was then Lent. Obviously, the Canadian abstained from more than the pleasures of the table at that time, and this could only have come about because they were heeding the precepts of their church.

W.J. Eccles

Notes

1. *Edits, Ordonnances Royaux, Déclarations et Arrêts du conseil d-Etat du Roi concernant le Canada* (Québec, 1854), p. 553.

2. Lucien Campeau S.I., ed., *Monumenta Novae Franciae I: 1602-1616* (Rome and Québec, 1967), pp. 4-5.

3. Marcel Trudel, *Histoire de la Nouvelle-France II: Le comptoir: 1604-1627* (Montréal, 1966), p. 91.

4. E.R. Adair, "France and the Beginnings of New France," *The Canadian Historical Review* 25 (Sept. 1944).

5. *Rapport de l'Archiviste de la Province de Québec,* Tome 41 (1963), pp. 109-10.

6. Dominion Bureau of Statistics, Demography Branch, "Chronological List of Canadian Censuses."

7. Jean Delumeau, *Le Catholicisme entre Luter et Voltaire* (Paris, 1971), pp. 256-57.

8. *Ibid.*

9. *Ibid.*
10. *Ibid.*, p. 270.
11. Louis Pérouas, *Le Diocèse de La Rochelle de 1648 à 1724, Sociologie et Pastorale* (Paris, 1964), p. 202.
12. Pierre Goubert, *The Ancien Regime: French Society, 1600-1750* (New York, 1974), p. 202.
13. Robert Mandrou, *Magistrats et sorciers en France au XVIIe siècle* (Paris, 1968).
14. Joyce Marshall, ed., *Word from New France: The Selected Letters of Marie de l'Incarnation* (Toronto, 1967).
15. Guy Grégault, *Le XVIIIe siècle canadien: Etudes* (Montréal, 1968), p. 105.
16. P.G. Roy, ed., *Inventaires des jugements et délibérations du Conseil Supérieur de la Nouvelle-France de 1717 à 1760*, 7 vols., (Beauceville, 1932-1935), 1:340-44, 346-47, 349-50.
17. Frégault, *Le XVIIIe siècle*, p. 88.
18. Noël Baillargeon, *Le Séminaire de Québec sous l'Episcopat de Mgr de Laval,* (Québec, 1972), pp. 52-55.
19. Archives Nationales, Paris, Series CIIA, Colonies 6:185, De Meulles au Ministre, Que., 4 nov. 1683.
20. Baillargeon, *Le Séminaire de Québec*, pp. 103-119.
21. *Ibid.*, p. 117; Marcel Trudel, *Initiation à la Nouvelle-France* (Montréal, 1968), pp. 255ff.
22. *Ibid.*
23. Henri-Raymond Casgrain, ed. *Collection des manuscrits du maréchal de Léevis*, 12 vols. (Montreal and Québec, 1889-1895), vol. 6, *Journal du Marquis de Montcalm durant ses campagnes au Canada de 1756 à 1760* (Québec, 1895), p. 61.
24. Trudel, *Initation*, p. 255ff.
25. Archives Nationales, Colonies, AN, CIIA 48:434, Jean Evesque de Québec au Ministre, Que. 10 Sept. 1726.
26. Archives Nationales, Colonies, Series CIIA 50:23-24, Beaucharnois et d'Aigremont au Ministre, Que. 1 oct. 1728.
27. P.G. Roy, *Inventaire des Ordonnances des intendants de la Nouvelle-France*, 3 vols. (Beauceville, 1917), 2:11; P.G. Roy, ed., *Inventaire des Jugements et délibérations du Conseil Souverain* (Québec, 1932-1935), 3:162; Archives du Séminaire de Quebec, polygraphie 6, no. 31.
28. Adolph Benson, ed., *Travels in North America by Peter Kalm*, 2 vols. (New York: Dover edition, 1966), 2:525.
29. Archives du Québec à Montréal, Greffe F. Simmonet, 1750.
30. Archives du Séminaire de Québec, polygraphie 6, no. 31.
31. Olwen H. Tufton, *The Poor of Eighteenth-Century France 1750-1789* (Oxford, 1974), p. 3.
32. Ibid., pp. 131-76.
33. Roy, *Ordonnances des Intendants*, passim; Archives Nationales, Colonies, Series B, 33:135; Ruette d'Auteil, *Mémoire de l'état présent du Canada* (1712).

34. Archives Nationales, Colonies, Series F3, 7:101, Moreau de Méry, "Hôspital à Montréal."

35. *Arrêts et Règlements du Conseil Supérieur de Québec, et Ordonnances et Jugements des intentants du Canada* (Québec, 1855), pp. 391-92.

36. On this institution, see Micheline D'Allaire, *L'Hôpital-Général de Québec 1692-1784* (Montréal, 1970).

37. Mgr. Henri Têtu, *Notices biographiques: Les Evèques de Québec* (Québec, 1889), p. 149.

38. Archives Nationales, Colonies, Series CIIA, vol. 27, "Abstraits des mémoires de Canada 1707," p. 59: *Nouvelle France: Documents Historiques: Correspondance échangée entre les authorités françaises et les gouverneurs et intendants* (Québec, 1893), 1:173.

39. Archives Nationales, Colonies, Series CIIA, 91:32 Galissonière et Bigot au Ministre, Que., 25 Sept. 1748.

40. W.J. Eccles, "Social Welfare Measures and Policies in New France," *XXXVI Congreso Internacional de Americanistas 4* (Sevilla, 1966).

41. *Edits, Ordonnances royaux, Déclarations et Arrêts du Conseil d'Etat du Roi concernant le Canada* (Québec, 1854), 1:288.

42. *Ordannances des Intendants et Arrêts portant règlements du Conseil Souverain* (Québec, 1806), 2:278-79.

43. Archives Ministère de la Guerre, Series A1-3417, no. 137, Montcalm au Ministre, Montréal, 12 juin 1756.

44. John McManners, *French Ecclesiastical Society under the Ancien Régime* (Manchester, 1960), pp. 92-102.

45. D'Allaire, *L'Hôpital-Général de Québec*, pp. 149-86.

46. *Rapport de l'Archiviste de la Province de Québec 1947-1948* Vaudreuil et Bégon au Ministre, Que. 12 nov. 1712, p. 185.

47. For a hostile description of Le Loutre's role, see Francis Parkman, *A Half Century of Conflict*, various editions.

48. Archives Nationales, Colonies, CIIA, vol. 26., Vaudreuil et Raudot au Ministre, Que. 15 nov 1707, p. 12; *Rapport de l'Archiviste de la Province de Québec 1939-1940*, p. 293.

49. Archives Nationales, Colonies, Series CIIA, 17:3ff, Callières et Champigny au Ministre, Que. 20 oct. 1699.

50. Archives du Québec à Montréal, Greffe Adhémar, no. 1350, 15 sept. 1724.

51. *Ibid.*, Greffe Baratée, no. 734, 22 dec. 1726; *Jugements et Délibérations du Conseil Souverain* 5:996-1000.

52. *Rapport de l'Archiviste de la Province de Québec 1947-1948*, p. 301; Archives Nationales, Colonies, Series CIIA 2:328; 18:64-66.

53. Archives du Québec à Montréal, Greffe J. David, no. 379, 31 juillet 1721.

54. Hufton, *The Poor*, p. 321, gives figures showing an almost threefold rise in the illegitimacy rate.

55. Archives Nationales, Colonies, Series CIIA 65:248-53.

56. See Hufton, *The Poor*, pp. 318-51; William L. Langer, "Checks on Population Growth: 1750-1850," *Scientific American*, Feb. 1972.

57. One finds innumerable *actes* for this form of adoption in the notarial *greffes*.

58. Jacques Henripin, *La population canadienne au début du XVIIIe siècle* (Paris, 1954).

The Philosophes and the
Psychology of Everyday Religion

The classical eighteenth-century document on the psychology of religion appeared in 1757: David Hume's essay on the *Natural History of Religion*. The text was preceded by a brief "Author's Introduction," largely prompted by fears of the formidable Bishop William Warburton, who threatened to enlist the attorney-general on the side of the gods. It should be read with the intonations of Hume's ambiguous intent, rather than in the bland manner in which it was assimilated by the innocent:

> As every enquiry, which regards religion, is of the utmost importance, there are two questions in particular, which challenge our attention, to wit, that concerning its foundation in reason, and that concerning its origin in human nature. Happily, the first question, which is the most important, admits of the most obvious, at least, the clearest, solution. The whole frame of nature bespeaks an intelligent author; and no rational enquirer can, after serious reflection, suspend his belief a moment with regard to the primary principles of genuine Theism and Religion. But the other question, concerning the origin of religion in human nature, is exposed to some more difficulty. [1]

Hume's distinction lies behind the topic I have chosen for this paper. It is not my object to discuss the philosophy of religion as it was formulated by major thinkers of the seventeenth and eighteenth centuries. I shall not be dealing with Spinoza's God, nor Herbert of Cherbury's God, nor Voltaire's God, nor Hume's wrestling with the idea of God in the suppressed *Dialogues concerning natural religion,* nor the militant refutations of the existence of God by Baron d'Holbach and the Marquis de Sade. I shall rather address myself to the second of Hume's questions, the origin of religion in human nature.

How did radical European writers in the eighteenth century explain the varieties of religious behaviour in the orthodox establishments, Catholic, Protestant and Jewish, with which they had immediate direct experience, as well as the behaviour of heathens in the worlds of savage and civilized paganism, knowledge of whose ceremonies had penetrated their consciousness through the reports of an ever-swelling volume of travel literature? The investigation of religious practice — recognized to be a virtually universal human phenomenon, despite a few isolated accounts of religionless savage peoples — led to the formulation of a psychology of religion, an explanation of mass behaviour, as distinct from the question of the truth or falsity of one or another belief. The documentation was vast: source materials could be collected from the literature of classical antiquity, from the church fathers, from the long parade of Christian heresies and sects, and juxtaposed with descriptions in heavy compendia of contemporary ceremonials. Without being burdened by the historicist preconceptions of the nineteenth century, the analysts of the eighteenth could breezily make comparisons, fix parallels, establish identities among specimens from all ages and places as if they were dealing with flora and fauna. The anti-clerical motives of many of the authors are patent: their psychology of religion was hardly a dispassionate science, and often diagnoses of fetish cults in Guinea (*vide* Charles de Brosses), or Ngombos in the Congo (*vide* Baron d'Holbach) or the deceiving mechanisms of Greek priests (*vide* Fontenelle) were really aimed at practices closer to home. But even if the underlying purpose was tainted, the method had at least the trappings of science. Evidence was assembled, hypotheses were framed (for example, Vico's and Hume's constructs of the emotions of primitive savages) and conclusions were reached. Antonius Van Dale meticulously examined the Old and New Testaments and rabbinic literature for the footprints of idolatry; Balthasar Bekker probed the travel literature of the nations for devil-worshippers. They were drawing up *catalogues raisonnés* of esoteric religious rituals, even as Presbyterian divines in mid-seventeenth-century England had compiled long catalogues of heresies and sectarian deviations.

I

There is no eighteenth-century book specifically entitled "The Psychology of Religion," though the term "psychology" had been around since Goclenius in the sixteenth century. Reflections on the subject, however, were strewn about in many different types of writing — natural histories of superstition, natural histories of religion, anatomies of religious melancholy and enthusiasm. Licentious novels depicted the psychological devastation wrought by religion on the inmates of monasteries and convents. Essays and books on education analyzed the psychic injuries inflicted on the young by prevailing popular religions. *Le Christianisme dévoilé* and *La Contagion sacrée* were characteristic titles from the atheist laboratory of the Baron d'Holbach, which treated all religion as pathological. But, strangely enough, by the end of the century many of the ideas first developed by the antagonists of religion had found their way into Christian apologetics; the emotive character of religion, once emphasized as a weakness, was suddenly turned into its primary virtue.

Describing and analyzing intimate religious experience are two seemingly different operations, though the division rarely is absolute. It is easier to maintain their separation when the functions are divided between two persons: one who does the experiencing, about which he leaves a record of sorts; the other who does the analysis, providing some external interpretation in terms of a psychological doctrine or perception. A few great psychologists of religious life, such as Saint Augustine, were capable of both processes; they were at least able to communicate something of the nature of their religious feeling even to outsiders.

In the eighteenth century most first-hand observers of other people's religious behaviour took a completely external view. They merely described ceremonial religious conduct and penetrated no further; at best they left laconic reports of the actors' general intent in engaging in certain performances. The explorers and priests who watched savage rites in various parts of the world tended to restrict themselves to silent pictures with a few stock captions such as "Hindus mourning the dead." Homebodies in Paris and London then tried to infuse these lifeless descriptions with meaning and became psychologists of religion after a fashion. True believers of course were, for the most part, untouched by this literature; they were satisfied that their own religion and its ceremonials had been revealed to their ancestors in the past and it was their duty to continue to believe and worship and obey commandments that could not be questioned. On occasion a particular ceremonial might be "explained" as interpretation. Yet even the most orthodox were drawn into the widely cast net of the eighteenth-century psychology of religion when they were confronted with aberrant religious behaviour in their midst.

Eighteenth-century thinkers ran some risks when they inquired directly into the origins of Judaism and Christianity or religion *tout court*. But since the most learned religious geographers of the seventeenth century, such as the antiquarian and astronomer Edward Brerewood, had estimated that at least five-sixths of the globe was inhabited by pagans and infidels, an extensive area of inquiry was open even to orthodox thinkers. Disbelievers, needless to add, gladly availed themselves of the cover of paganism, ancient and modern. Moreover, within the Christian lands of Europe there were a number of types of religious behaviour which, since the Renaissance and the Reformation, could be diagnosed without incurring official censure. For example, in Protestant countries the saint-worship and monasticism of Catholic countries could be identified with pagan rituals, and these could be discussed as pathological or diabolical phenomena. Among both Protestants and Catholics, fanatical "enthusiasm" and mystical pretensions, always regarded uneasily in orthodox establishments, could be treated as religious pathology that required the understanding of physicians as well as clergymen. Granted that such behaviour was inspired by demons, from the Renaissance on it was legitimate to enquire into the mechanics that they used in gaining possession of their victims. This, too, opened the door to naturalistic analyses, especially in connection with the trial of witches.

Eighteenth-century thinkers who treated the critical study of popular religion among the ancients with the respect due to ancestors had inherited a body of basic conceptions and theories. Lucretius and Lucian were favourites of the age. Moralists, such as Cicero, had already distinguished between a philosophical belief in the gods and popular religion and had analyzed both. But one must not forget the church fathers as rich source books of analysis of pagan behaviour. Voltaire was deeply immersed in patristic literature, as is evident from even a cursory examination of the books he owned (now in Leningrad) and their marginalia; and the church fathers, in fighting the abominable rites of pagans, Gnostics and heretics, had left lurid commentaries on religious practices, which could be adapted to serve the purposes of eighteenth-century anti-clerical unveilers of the secret springs of all religion. Euhemeristic explanations of the pagan gods as mere kings who had divinized themselves — a favourite form of interpretation among the learned in the seventeenth and eighteenth centuries, for whom it provided much academic employment — had, after all, been transmitted to modern times primarily through the polemics of the church fathers against the reality of the pagan gods.

Time-worn religious problems within monotheistic religions, as well as the unmasking of paganism in antiquity, nourished eighteenth-century writers with ideas on the psychological nature of religion itself. The *philosophes* were not averse to learning from their enemies. One of the oldest concerns of Judaism and Christianity, for example, was how to distinguish between true and false prophecy. The medieval Jewish philosopher Maimonides had devoted large parts of a number of his treatises to tests for discovering a false prophet. By the seventeenth century, his reasoning had been absorbed into the Christian world, and especially in England and Holland there grew up a voluminous literature that concentrated on the signs whereby fanatical pretenders to direct communication with God could be detected. Burton's *Anatomy of Melancholy* of 1621 included a large section on religious melancholy, by which he meant religious manias in all times and places. His express purpose was to differentiate *true* religion from superstitious and pathological behaviour. Materials from his treatise were picked up by two early-eighteenth-century Whig pamphleteers, John Trenchard and Thomas Gordon. Trenchard wrote a *Natural History of Superstition*, which was reflected in Hume's *Natural History of Religion* in the middle of the century, and finally in Holbach's *La Contagion sacrée, ou histoire naturelle de la superstition* in 1768. Holbach posed simply as a translator of Trenchard and Gordon, but he really used their names and a small section of their work to lend weight to his own exposition of atheism and to development of his unique psychology of religion. We have here an example of how an orthodox religious preoccupation, the differentiation between true and false prophecy, could ultimately end up in a clinical study of all religion as a disease.

Thus eighteenth-century writers, when they analyzed popular religious behaviour, were hardly ploughing in virgin soil. To be sure, they knew the classical studies better than the works of Renaissance and Reformation doctors such as Girolame Cardano and Johann Wier and Peter van Foreest. As was the manner of the age, they often reiterated old ideas as if they were totally new discoveries and they put forth a number of propositions for which one can surely find hints and origins in previous literature and which they merely presented in greater detail. But they also introduced novel conceptions. The polemical purpose of their work lent passion to their writing, and the arguments of their predecessors infiltrated European thought of later ages in the form that the *philosophes* gave them.

In the course of this paper I shall not presume to dwell on all aspects of the eighteenth-century psychology of religion but shall confine myself to a few of its basic principles. It should be taken for granted that I am looking for common denominators and make no pretence to a proper evaluation of any individual thinker's view. The sworn enemies of the *esprit de système* left no co-ordinated body of reflections on the subject that preoccupied them perhaps more than any other: how could man, capable of reason, descend to the childishness, cruelty and madness of most religious practices? My presentation may bestow more of a structure on their thought than they would have accepted; and while hypostasizing an eighteenth-century body of radical thought on the psychology of religion, I am well aware of the great diversity of opinion among writers and the frequent contradictions within them. We are, after all, dealing with *philosophes*, not philosophers.

Fear of God, the Yrat Ha-shem, Fear of the Name, of the rabbis, was traditionally one of the loftiest attributes of the religious man. For some Reformation theologians, *Gottesfurcht* became the pivot of religious belief. Among the eighteenth-century *philosophes*, fear of God was transformed into a negative trait of the religious personality, the presumed source of much that was stupid, cruel and self-destructive in religious behaviour.

Popular religion, with its major premise that God had a special concern for the particular of each individual, was for most *philosophes* the product of man's anxiety, which took the form of exaggerating fears of the future as well as hopes for the future. On balance, fear predominated over hope in the emotional equipment of men, and the ancient Lucretian dictum that in the beginning the gods were born of fear was reaffirmed. The eighteenth century added a number of elements to this basic psychological theory. Since the experience of fear was not isolated but tended to involve and draw along other emotions, fear gave rise to a whole complex of behaviour patterns. Fear brought men to such a state of anxiety that they lost their rational faculties and jumped at any prospect or promise of removing the cause of fear or mitigating the punishment and pain they dreaded. They behaved towards gods as they would towards more powerful men they encountered. The Baron d'Holbach invented the neologism "anthropomorphism" to describe the projection of human emotion into the gods, before whom men cringed as if they were angry, exigent, out-sized human beings. Fear-stricken believers turned over money and goods and choice objects to fakir priests, who offered them alleviation of pain in this world and reduction of pain in the next. Sometimes fear was so great that men sacrificed their children and inflicted punishment on themselves, in monstrous violation of the natural pleasure-principle, in order to forestall some greater punishment threatened by the raging, unseen gods. Men had to give conspicuous proof of denying themselves pleasure and tormenting themselves spiritually and physically until they reached the point of madness. So limitless was their fear of the infinite God they had invented that they even sacrificed a god to appease his fury, an Holbachian conceit that Nietzsche later adopted without benefit of citation.

Fear and self-denial created a sour temper, a mean disposition, which induced aggressive and cruel conduct. In monotheism the power of one God was maximized and fear of him was so consuming — as contrasted with the division of spheres of influence among the myriad gods of polytheism — that the monotheist believer tended to be the most timorous of creatures and the most cruel to enemies of the religion upon which he was fixated. David Hartley's doctrine of association, expounded in the *Observations on Man* (1749), an idea common enough in various guises in eighteenth-century thought, made this constant overflow of the emotion of fear into all aspects of existence quite plausible. Emotions set off sympathetic vibrations just as musical instruments did, Hume taught.

Such thinking carried *philosophes* to the deduction that there were parallel scales in the gradations of natural fear and superstitious behaviour. Those persons who were weakest, either by nature or as a consequence of their situation in the world, were, experience showed, the most frightened. Travel literature, as Hume read it, revealed to him the spectacle of the savage terrified because the manifest uncertainties of nature made his existence miserable and precarious, subject to sudden, violent cataclysms before which he was helpless. Vico's primitives were overwhelmed by the shock of thunder and lightning after the post-diluvian drying-out of the earth, and they never recovered from their initial terror. Sailors whose condition placed them in constant dread of drowning were naturally more superstitious than other men. Women and children and the aged were given to religious superstition and suffered from grossly exaggerated fears because of their unprotected state.

Men were so prone to forge into absolute bonds chance coincidences of association that if the sight of an insect, beast or plant accompanied misfortune, they would ever afterwards be afraid of it, and in order to placate, they would soon come to worship the thing, irrespective of how vile it might be. This helped men as widely separated in temperament as the président de Brosses and the Baron d'Holbach to account for the fetichism of Africa and the Egyptian adoration of animals. Weak-minded savages who could not reason fell easy victim to such associations, but even ordinary people in civilized countries made similar connections. Response depended on their emotional state, they had learned from Spinoza, the secret master of the *philosophes*. In health and good spirits, a man paid no attention to counsel; in the dire straits of misfortune, he flung himself upon the first bystander and begged for advice. Sickness and the catastrophes that overwhelmed all men, civilized and primitive, made them turn to gods for succour.

A corollary of the fear theory bred a measure of hopefulness, even among sceptical philosophers, such as Hume. In a state of civility, where fears were somewhat diminished because of the relative security of urban living — oh, *tempora mutantur!* — men became a bit less timorous, hence less superstitious, that is, less prone to believe in false causes and effects and, to follow out the chain of rational consequences, less fanatical in their religion. But Hume had little faith that the mass of mankind, and even the philosopher most of the time, would ever be free from the anxieties inspired by the fear of death; hence the end of superstition and the superstitious religion was not to be expected.

The outright atheist Holbach was sometimes more sanguine. Through the progress of the human man — and he used the phrase "*les progrès de l'esprit humain*" as early as 1758 — it could be proved to men that there were no gods. Under atheism, fear of the gods and all its noxious consequences would be banished and men would be naturally happier.

But members of the Holbach circle, such as the young engineer Nicolas Boulanger, were not quite as confident of the future as Holbach himself. For Boulanger, the fears and sadness expressed in the myths and ceremonies of all religions were the reactions of the survivors of the deluges that periodically inundated the earth. All religions were for him repetitive transmissions of accounts of a deluge. They were uniformly lugubrious, the litanies of victims who were traumatized, psychologically driven to repeat over and over again the tale of their suffering in poetic and symbolic forms, even as you and I never weary of recounting the tale of some misfortune. Since periodic catastrophes were inevitable, this religion of fear and mourning would be constantly renewed, though in the enlightened stages of a civilization's cycle, in the interim before the next deluge, knowledge of the origin of religious emotion might liberate men from total enthralment to its superstitions.

Vico's theory of religion, which also held that religion was born of fear, moved in a very different direction. Fear and terror, felt by the feral beings who first identified the god of thunder as a fellow-creature with superior powers, were still the forces that dominated human action at every critical moment in world history. But for Vico, terror was the instrumentality of the civilizing process, and the self-denial demanded by the god triggered off a chain of events that culminated in the principal civil institutions of society.

The overwhelming number of *philosophes* who rooted the popular religions in fear saw them as destructive of human happiness. Diderot was perhaps the most persuasive of the psychologists of fear-religion when he dwelt on its distortion of human personality. In a wild excursion in one of his *Salons* he wickedly raised the possibility of another religion, an alternative to Christianity, with its apotheosis of fear and suffering, which Holbach called the religion of a *dieu pauvre et crucifié*. Diderot scandalously suggested that if Western culture had inherited a Christ who had had an affair with the Magdalene and at a joyous wedding-banquet in Cana, between two wines, "had caressed the breasts of a bridesmaid and the buttocks of Saint John," a spirit of delight would have spread throughout all the adherents of this sensuous religion.[2]

In a few passages the Baron d'Holbach in his lumbering way tried to look behind the fear syndrome of mankind and to ask forthrightly why the creature was so frightened. The run of *philosophes* operated on the premise that terror of death was the ultimate emotion, which required no further explanation. Holbach ventured to suggest that the ubiquity of this fear, which engendered a belief in a deity, demanded deeper probing. Man feared because he was naturally necessitous, and from the first moment of his existence there were others about who could satisfy the needs he made known through cries of pain. This reliance upon "the others who were stronger," usually his parents, became deeply ingrained in his nature, and when he grew to adulthood the dependence upon an almighty god to satisfy his needs and allay his pains was fortified by the "remembrance" (the word is Holbach's) of his infantile state of utter helplessness.

In many areas the radical materialist *philosophes* introduced a time-dimension into their psychological systems — the perseveration of first memories of childhood, the fixation upon the early catastrophes of the race that then became embedded in myths and religious rites, the power of error transmitted from primitive times through habit and custom. The *philosophes* believed, of course, that enlightenment could break the historical bonds that fettered mankind of one generation to another — or at least might weaken them.

If the psychologists' domino theory was credited, then fear led to psychic suffering on the part of the religious adept, the suffering brought on a concealed rage, and the rage vented itself in cruel persecution of heretics and unbelievers. Instead of religion being viewed as the solace of mankind, this sacred disease was seen as the source of the greatest miseries. Again, it was Diderot, in his novel *La Religieuse*, who illustrated the sexual perversities and cruelties generated in the unnatural atmosphere of a convent, where women in the name of religious devotion denied themselves the fulfilment of elementary passions. The fear of God drove them to the extremes of absurdity and madness; they lacerated their own flesh in exercises that baffled most of the *philosophes* and to which their subtlest reasoning could offer no clue. Trenchard, in his natural history of superstition, did show an awareness that some kinds of religious self-punishment — specifically monks' "scarifying their backsides" — might in fact produce sexual pleasure. But such allusions to flagellation as a means of sexual gratification were rare. In general, self-inflicted tortures as part of religious observance were considered inexplicable lunacy and dismissed at that.

That asceticism was unnatural and ascetic practices brought about consequences opposite to those intended had frequently been remarked upon by doctors of the Renaissance, and no less a man than Isaac Newton condemned the practices of anchorites who, in their futile attempts to banish lewd and lascivious images from their minds, were only driven to dwell on them the more. One of his religious manuscripts disserted this predicament with insight:

> Desire was inflamed by prohibition of lawful marriage, and...the profession of chastity and daily fasting on that account put them perpetually in mind of what they strove against...By immoderate fasting the body is also put out of its due temper and for want of sleep and fancy is invigorated about what ever it sets itself upon and by degrees inclines towards a delirium in so much that those Monks who fasted most arrived to a state of seeing apparitions of women and other shapes...in such a lively manner as made them often think the visions true apparitions of the Devil tempting them to lust.[3]

Similar psychological diagnosis of chimeras consequent upon what we would today call sensory deprivation can be found among many of the *philosophes*. That an overscrupulous punitive censor provokes a rebellious id is, of course, a commonplace among present-day clinicians.

II

One of the psychological bases of the eighteenth-century distinction between true philosophical religion and popular religion lay in a dogmatic opinion about the nature of perception among primitives. Many of the missionaries to the heathen, both Catholic and Protestant, in trying to explain away their lack of success in making converts, resorted to the excuse that primitive peoples had no capacity for abstract ideas, a notion that had wide currency in seventeenth and eighteenth-century anthropology and that lived on well into the twentieth century, until it was discredited by Claude Lévi-Strauss. This attempt of the international salesmen of religion to justify to the home office their own incompetence was in line with the opinions of the *philosophes* about the psychic incapacity of the ordinary people, Christian or heathen, to reach the exalted level of members of the Academy, either in religion or in philosophy. In his early reflections on religion, John Locke had explained idol and saint-worship as a result of the almost ineradicable tendency of common people to concretize. Savages knew the names of objects, not of abstract qualities, and for ordinary people God had to be portrayed in a manner comprehensible to the senses. In Locke's wake, David Hume saw that most men could not maintain themselves on the abstract level of monotheism but had to fall back, like the tides, into polytheistic doctrines in which each god had a particular control over a specific natural element that was associated with him. Catholic saints played the same role — they were tailored to fit the perceptual capacities and understanding of ordinary humans. Calvinist fire-and-brimstone sermons had to reify the torments of hell in order to be effective. Popular religion, pagan or Christian, in all times and places was likely to be cursed with the same concreteness. The people were incapable of reasoning through a long linkage of causes and effects to a primary cause; they had to make up some immediate tangible cause, a saint's image or a relic, and impute to it powers it did not possess.

The same generalization that *philosophes* had made about gradation in the fear syndrome was repeated with respect to concreteness of perception: the more ignorant a person (a child, for example), the less his capacity for abstraction. What applied to the individual had occurred in the history of the race: benighted savages concretized; higher stages of civilization acquired a capacity for abstraction. Women were likely to have less aptitude for abstraction and to be more addicted to superstitious religions (an idea that has become taboo in my lifetime).

Again, even the philosopher had only partially outgrown this deficiency. When he donned his philosophical robes and thought rigorously and scientifically he might, for a time, be emancipated from the concreteness syndrome. But in ordinary, everyday life he too was subject to making concrete analogies and failed to display the abstract capacity necessary for a philosophical religion. Some of the deists had a rather crude physiological conception of why men did not hold firm by the innate idea of God with which they believed all human beings were endowed. It seems that primitives had soft brains, and erroneous impressions could readily write themselves thereon and distort their natural, pure reason, making them a prey to imaginary monsters. False religion was thus an off-shoot of the physio-psychology of error.

In the latter part of the eighteenth century a number of theories on the origins of religion assumed a more sophisticated shape. Charles Dupuis' *Origine de tous les cultes* (1795), in a revival of ancient Stoic doctrines and seventeenth-century ideas, saw prac-tical religion, including Christianity, as a degenerate form of scientific knowledge about the universe. The masses, because they could not remain on the requisite high level of true theory about the nature of things, corrupted the findings of ancient philoso-phers and, like the Egyptians, fell to worshipping animals and other low things whose symbolic meaning they could no longer read. The idea of religion as primitive science opened the possi-bility of a new, true religion of science, a conception with a long future history.

Another idea that looked to the future was the sexual inter-pretation of religion. After the introduction of epics from India, along with Indian sculpture, there was a minor attempt to dis-cover the genesis of religion in a symbolic rendering of human sexual activity. (There had been ancient doctrines to this effect.) But while this inspired some pornographic interest in collecting certain types of Greek and Roman coins, it was not a widely dif-fused psychological scheme of interpretation.

III

There were eighteenth-century thinkers who, while committed to the idea that popular religion had its origins in fear, held that this was necessary for the maintenance of the state and civil soci-ety. In a variation of the ancient Critias doctrine, they contended that fear of the gods prevented men from committing secret crimes and thus served the interests of the state by helping to maintain order. Voltaire's "footman's religion" was tinctured with psychology — though the forthright atheist Holbach shocked his contemporaries with the assertion that it was the state's gallows and not the gods that deterred men from crime.

In its most militant form, anti-clerical analysis of religion, while it subscribed to the fear theory and the idea of the ordinary man's incapacity for abstract thought, tended to concentrate on the lust for power as the most compelling drive behind the propa-gation and maintenance of institutional religions. The power-lust could be imputed either to kings or cliques of priests, who conspired to impose deceptions and false beliefs on the mass of people. Not all individuals were equally wily and power-hungry. Most of the guileless merely did as they were told by the more astute, who acted out of self-interest, that eighteenth-century theoretical jack-of-all-trades. There were mastery and riches and pleasure to be gained by those who directed the religious plot and enforced a monopoly of knowledge for themselves while they kept the people in darkness. This plot theory of the origins and sustenance of religion was shared by Voltaire and Holbach and received its final form in Condorcet's *Esquisse*. Ordinary people acted out of habit. Once their ancestors had been instructed by priests about the commandments of the gods, they were transmitted from generation to generation and remained unaltered, except when a few extraordinary persons broke through the shell of custom and made an attempt to perceive relationships freshly. It was then that priests in alliance with tyrants moved to destroy the heretics who had brought new perceptions into the world, and the mass of the people, terrified of suffering a similar fate, continued their religious performances like docile sheep. Through their monopoly of knowledge, the priests not only could amass wealth and power but, while preaching ascetic behaviour to the people, could enjoy all manner of sexual gratification for themselves. Seventeenth and eighteenth-century stories — Denis Vairasse's *History of the Sevarambians*, for example — featured wicked priests who forced innocent virgins into sexual relations by making them believe they were having converse with a god. The sexual advantages gained by priests through knowledge imparted in the confessional became a stereotype of the anti-clerical crusade. Ordinary human stupidity, played upon by the craftiness of a few tyrants and their priestly cohorts, offered a complete explanation of most religious behaviour. "In a word," Holbach pontificated in *La Contagion sacrée*, "sovereigns had to rule by prejudice backed up by force. Caprice was their only law, a power without limits the object of their desires. And having become the cruelest enemies of their peoples they had to look for supernatural means to hold them in subjection, to prevent them from resisting the evils that they endured...Only religion could perform these miracles."[4]

IV

Most of the theories of the psychology of religion that I have touched upon thus far were advanced by the enemies of revealed religion. Often, as we have seen, the same doctrines that were developed in the seventeenth century to distinguish true religion from fanatical enthusiasm were taken over intact or adapted by the eighteenth century as a battering ram against the whole orthodox religious structure of society. In the second half of the century, however, a new view of religion sprang up among a number of seminal writers that was, so to speak, a negation of the eighteenth-century negation. Rousseau, Hamann and Herder, and also orthodox Catholic apologists in France, viewed religious performances in a new, positive light, and to bolster this changed attitude towards popular and even institutional religion a new psychology of religion was evolved.

The meaning of Rousseau's religion is open to a wide variety of interpretations, but in one of its aspects it introduced great novelty. For Rousseau, unlike Montesquieu, religion in its very essence was not to be understood as a social utility; nor was it a historical phenomenon that at best had served to mollify the cruelty of barbarian invaders, as Edward Gibbon at one point contended; nor was it merely a necessary bridle or restraint on the wild concupiscence and inherent evil nature of man, as the orthodox apologists of all religions believed. Religion was an expansive effusion of the human emotions of love and benevolence, which represented the best in man's nature. Rousseau's Vicar of Savoy saw religion as the mainspring of virtuous feeling and action. Religion was a vital part of the education of man because it brought to the fore his naturally benign sentiments. It was a positive drive, a *ressort*, not a mere *frein*. This religion of the heart needed no elaborate institutional forms, could be inspired in man by the beauties of nature and, far from being the special province of the learned and the scientific, had its greatest chances of development in the natural feelings of untutored peasants. The Vicar exhorted Emile: "Behold the spectacle of nature; listen to the inner voice. Has not God spoken it all to our eyes, to our conscience. . ."[5] The whole Rousseauistic conception of human nature fostered this simple religious belief. Only aristocrats and corrupted savants were atheists. The religion of the people was natural and spontaneous — at least before it was spoiled by arts and sciences.

On the eve of the Revolution, this Rousseauistic religion, strangely enough, penetrated the works of official popular Catholic apologists, and ceremonials were devised that harmonized with this conception of religious belief as a positive stimulus to virtue. The spreading cult of the rose wreath, in which villagers, by general consent, awarded a prize of virtue to a local virgin — a ceremony attended by the lord, the clergy and royal officials — was a manifestation of this new view that among the peasantry of France true religious feeling was still alive, whatever might be happening in the salons. "I feel within me the love of the good and I give myself up to it," preached the Abbé Vourlet de Vauxcelles, a court cleric sent up to Normandy to participate in a rose wreath fete. The very titles of popular works of apologetics gave evidence that a new psychology of religion was in the making. The Abbé Adrien Lamourette — the later initiator of a kissing game during one tense revolutionary assembly — had published in 1788 *Les Délices de la religion*.

Catholic apologetics, as if in answer to the arguments of those psychologists who saw religion as born of fear or religion as a consequence of power-lust or religion as an attribute of brutish ignorance, were propagating a new, romantic view of religion as the natural spontaneous gift of all good and feeling people. This may have been a last-ditch attempt of the compromised church of the Cardinal de Rohan to save itself, but it turned out to be a prefiguration of a whole new psychological interpretation of religious behaviour that was to flourish in the nineteenth century and is far from dead today. Whether this facile, sentimentalized religion bears any but the most tenuous relatonship to the scriptural and historical religions of Judaism and Christianity is, as my master Hume would say, "exposed to some more difficulty."

Though related to Rousseauism, the interpretation of religion that was being prepared on the other side of the Rhine by one of the fathers of German Romanticism, Johann Gottfried Herder, opened an entirely new mode for understanding the genesis and worth of religion in civilization. Instead of being an evil growth it again became the heart of culture. As part of his philosophico-historical outline of the history of the *Volk*, Herder saw the birth of the religion of a people as its most spontaneous creative moment. Responding to the inspiration of the physical environment in which it was created, religion was the primal molder of a national soul, the wellspring of its whole history. To be sure, Montesquieu had conceived of religion as a vital element in fashioning the spirit of a nation, but in his rationalist frame religious creativity was not endowed with anything like the preponderance of a driving force, which Herder granted it. This new psychological view of religion that was nourished in the Germanic world was a militant denial of the accumulated theories that English philosophers and French *philosophes* had developed in the course of the eighteenth century. When Hume's *Natural History of Religion* was translated into German, Herder quickly picked it up and focused on the sceptical philosopher's admission that religious emotion was spontaneous. Hume had marked it a secondary emotion, derivative from fear; Herder rejected the fear theory and stressed the sentiment itself. When Herder read Boulanger's reconstruction of the origins of religious ritual, he ridiculed it as a *wassertheologie*. He stood on their heads all the psychological perceptions of the *philosophes*. And religion, instead of being the major source of human depredations and cruelties, became the font of all creativity in art and literature.

Thus, in the course of the century, the psychology of ordinary religion had been shifted from an offensive weapon against established religion to a bulwark of Christianity.

Frank E. Manuel

Notes

1. David Hume, *The Natural History of Religion,* ed. H.E. Toot (London, 1956), p. 21.

2. Denis Diderot, *Oeuvres complètes*, ed. J. Assezat and M. Tourneux (Paris, 1875-77), 10:492-93.

3. Jerusalem, Jewish National and University Library, Yahuda MS. 18.1, vol. 2; quoted in F.E. Manuel, *The Religion of Isaac Newton* (Oxford, 1974), p. 13.

4. Paul-Henri Thiry, Baron d'Holbach, *Textes choisis*, ed. Paulette Charbonnel (Paris, 1957), p. 158.

5. Jean-Jacques Rousseau, *Emile* (Everyman edition), p. 259.

Wesley and the
Renewal of English Religion

John Wesley has not been the victim of undue neglect. It might be claimed, indeed, that he has suffered from an excess of adulation, and that this has fostered an uncritical interpretation of the man and his work. It is often assumed that he was unique; he was not, though he was clearly exceptional. There were other reactions to the aridity which afflicted so much of mid-eighteenth-century religion. Howell Harris in Wales, Samuel Walker in Cornwall, William Grimshaw in Yorkshire all represent stirrings of religious life comparable with, but clearly distinguishable from, Methodism.[1] The very fact that others were pursuing the same end makes it important to examine Wesley's relation to the age in which he lived.

It is worth recalling that Wesley was probably more familiar with more aspects of eighteenth-century life than most of his contemporaries. He was incessantly on the move at a time when travel was always slow and difficult and often dangerous. Most educated men of the time were familiar with London, Oxford or Cambridge, and a provincial town or a country parish. The places that Wesley visited read like a gazetteer of Great Britain. Moreover, he was a shrewd and perceptive observer, and he noted down his reactions to what he saw. Consequently his *Journal* is a social document of unique interest. From few other sources can the student learn so much about daily life in the less frequented parts of the country. Sometimes, of course, Wesley found himself in the midst of events of great historical importance. In September 1745 he was in Newcastle-upon-Tyne when the Jacobite army, having captured Edinburgh, was poised for its march southwards. It was uncertain whether the Young Pretender would choose the western route through Carlisle or the eastern one through Newcastle. He chose the former, but there were anxious days in Newcastle, and Wesley gives a vivid account of the city's preparations as it braced itself to check the anticipated onset of the Highland Host.[2]

Wesley was a sympathetic observer of the eighteenth century because he shared many of its presuppositions. By similarity, as well as by contrast, he provides an excellent standard by which to judge the period. He was, of course, an unsparing critic of the shortcomings of the Church of England, especially of the complacency, the worldliness, the indifference of many of the clergy. These men were oblivious of the corruptions in the Church because they were a part of them. By ignoring the spread of practical paganism, they were betraying their trust. But he never dreamt of forsaking the Church, and he insisted that his followers should not do so either.

He was equally critical of and loyal to that very clerical society, the University of Oxford. For many years he faithfully discharged the duties of a college tutor. On a visit to St. Andrew's, he discovered that the students were on holiday, and he was shocked. How different from his teaching days! "I should have thought myself little better than a highwayman," he wrote, "if I had not lectured them every day of the year but Sundays."[3] He was aware of the presence of the "college drones" whom Gibbon pilloried so mercilessly in his famous description of the fellows of Magdalen. He had nothing but contempt for the "wretch who has received ten talents, and employs none; that is not only promised a reward, but is also paid beforehand for his work, and yet works not at all." He was aware of the "drowsy ingratitude, the lazy perjury" of some who had found refuge in college common rooms.[4] But he regularly identified himself in his works as a fellow (present or past) of Lincoln College, Oxford. These two institutions (the Church and the university) clearly set their stamp upon him; they helped to make him what he was: an eighteenth-century Englishman.

Wesley would be inconceivable in any other period. The calm reasonableness of his mind, the closely argued structure of his works, even the cool lucidity of his style, all belong to the eighteenth century. It was suspected by some of his contemporaries, and it has been assumed by many of their successors, that his reaction against the shortcomings of his age had led him to renounce its most salient characteristic — its reliance on reason. Uncritical readers noted that in the most famous passage in his works (his account of his Aldersgate "conversion") he had stated that his "heart was strangely warmed."[5] This has often been interpreted as a predominantly emotional reaction against the rationalism of the age. But though his heart was strangely warmed, his head remained remarkably cool. Religion is concerned with the whole man; because Wesley had discovered the importance of feeling, he did not feel obliged to minimize the significance of thought.

It is true that his critics believed that he had abandoned reason as well as common sense. This exposed him to what the age regarded as the most damaging of all charges: he was accused of being an "enthusiast." In eighteenth-century usage, "enthusiasm" was a blanket term of abuse used to cover all forms of fanaticism. Any exceptional ardour invited the charge; so did a display of conviction about beliefs that lay beyond the pale of conventional orthodoxy. Wesley seemed particularly vulnerable to this charge. In the early instalments of the *Journal* he recorded a series of episodes that outraged every canon of eighteenth-century propriety. Wesley himself was puzzled; his friend Whitefield and his brother Charles were shocked at the reports and hastened to remonstrate. These strange phenomena are a perplexing feature of the Revival. They occurred at one place (Bristol), only in the early stages of the movement, and only in connection with the preaching of John Wesley himself. It is clear that he did nothing to encourage these manifestations. Later he was inflexible in his opposition to anything remotely akin to them. When Thomas Maxfield, one of his assistants, showed a disposition to foster emotionalism, Wesley reprimanded him in the most emphatic terms. He was satisfied that he himself was not guilty of what he, like all his contemporaries, regarded as a deplorable fault. "I believe thinking men," he wrote, "mean by *enthusiasm* a sort of religious madness; *a false imagination* of being inspired by God. And by an *enthusiast* one that fancies himself under the influence of the Holy Ghost, when, in fact, he is not. Let him prove me guilty of this who can."[6] But to define the fault and repudiate it did not silence the critics. He was exposed to blame as long as he preached with fervour, and inevitably his strong convictions translated themselves into an earnestness which his sophisticated contemporaries could neither overlook nor forgive. In October 1766 Horace Walpole heard Wesley preach before a congregation in Bath, and he commented on his cleanliness, his oratory — and his enthusiasm. "There were parts and eloquence in his sermon," he wrote, "but towards the end he exalted his voice and acted very ugly enthusiasm."[7] In the Bath of Beau Nash, Wesley could expect no other verdict.

It was widely assumed that any man exposed to the charge of "enthusiasm" must be a person suspicious of reason. On this score Wesley felt that he was beyond the reach of criticism. He believed that his *Appeals to Men of Reason and Religion* represented his most convincing defence of his movement. To his mind there was nothing incongruous in the titles of these works. In order to appeal to men on behalf of religion it was necessary to convince their minds. Nor was he content to leave his readers to draw this inference for themselves. He explicitly denied that there was any necessary incompatibility between his intelligence and his beliefs. He could not countenance a divorce between faith and reason. "I am for both," he said; "for faith to perfect my reason, that by the Spirit of God not putting out the eyes of my understanding but enlightening them more and more, I may 'be ready to give a clear,' scriptural 'answer to every man that asketh me a reason for the hope that is in me.'"[8] He insisted that he preached "a religion evidently founded on and every way agreeable to, eternal reason, to the essential nature of things."[9] This was an aspect of his defence which he developed with all the cogency that a former lecturer in logic could command. "We therefore not only allow, but earnestly exhort all who seek after true religion to use all the reason which God hath given them, in seeking out the things of God."[10]

This alliance of faith and reason made it possible for him to be unyielding in his adherence to certain beliefs and yet very flexible in his attitude towards others. For example, he believed in the truths enunciated in the doctrine of the Trinity, but he was not prepared to contend with fellow-Christians about the form in which that doctrine should be expressed. The one was a matter of conviction, the other of opinion. "We do not lay the main stress of our religion on any opinions, right or wrong; neither do we ever begin, or willingly join in, any dispute concerning them." "I will not quarrel with you," he added, "about any opinion."[11]

This reflects an accommodating approach; it does not imply indefinite beliefs. As a matter of fact, Wesley worked out a very serviceable pattern of theology. He had a useful doctrine of authority, which started with the Bible, as illuminated by the Holy Spirit, interpreted by reason, confirmed by personal experience and fortified by the testimony of other Christians. His system began with man where he is — in trouble — and explained this by appealing to the fact of original sin. But a sinner will not heed the gospel, so prevenient grace breaks in to arrest attention; then, as man sees himself in his misery, he responds by repenting, receives forgiveness, is justified by faith and begins the long process of sanctification. The "new birth" was vitally important to Wesley; so was the witness of the Spirit, and it all culminated in that central but elusive Wesleyan doctrine, Christian perfection.

This theology provided the substance of Wesley's preaching, and preaching, it must be remembered, was the means of evangelizing on which he chiefly relied. The modern reader is impressed at once by the massive structure and the close reasoning of Wesley's sermons and marvels at their reported effectiveness. They bear no relation whatsoever to anything that our age would recognize as popular preaching. To Wesley's contemporaries the puzzling feature was not the content but the method. They assumed, as Wesley did originally, that a sermon could only appropriately be preached in a church. But when he began to proclaim a revitalized faith, he found that one by one the church doors were shut against him. Then his friend Whitefield made a novel suggestion: if he could not preach in the churches, why not preach in the open air? With considerable reluctance he agreed. "At four o'clock in the afternoon," he wrote, "I submitted to be more vile, and proclaimed in the highways the glad tidings of salvation, speaking from a little eminence to about three thousand people."[12] That could hardly be described as a discouraging start, and Wesley soon discovered that almost anywhere, at almost any hour, he could attract audiences that could be numbered only in the thousands. The *Journal* is full of vivid glimpses of that ministry — for example, of Wesley preaching at night in a thunder storm, when he could see the upturned faces of his congregation only when the lightning lit them up for a moment; or of a crowd of miners pausing as they came off shift to listen to him, and as the story of salvation unfolded the tears began to cut white channels through the coal dust on their cheeks. When that happens, the preacher can be assured that he is reaching his hearers. They may not seem the effect you might expect from the sermons as we have them in published form. How did Wesley, a middle-aged Oxford don, achieve such results? But, of course, he did not realize that in preaching to coal miners and others he had a problem of communication. He simply preached, and they simply responded.

In the arts of pure oratory, Wesley was clearly inferior to George Whitefield, but his abiding influence proved to be infinitely greater. The secret of his success lay in his ability to conserve his results. He undoubtedly had exceptional organizing ability. He gathered his followers into societies. Subsequently he divided them into "classes." Both provided what we would now call "systems of support." They afforded the new convert direction, oversight, encouragement and opportunities for growth. A person who showed capacity could rise step by step through the stages of an emerging hierarchy of offices and might end as one of Wesley's preachers. There was assistance for those who had problems, as well as for those who gave promise. Wesley inaugurated a loan fund to help people improve their position, dispensaries for the poor, schools, orphanages and other remedial agencies. Social service went hand in hand with evangelism. Wesley could recognize and implement a good idea, but he did not necessarily originate it. Whitefield suggested open-air preaching. Initially Wesley was as strongly opposed to preaching by laymen as he was to preaching out-of-doors. He had assigned certain limited functions to his lay assistants, but he certainly did not intend to let them preach. When Thomas Maxfield began to preach in his absence, Wesley came flying back to London to check this irregularity. But his mother, who was living with him at the Foundery,[13] raised a disconcerting question. How could he be sure, she asked, that Maxfield was not as truly called of the Holy Ghost to preach as he himself was? At all events, she added, he ought to suspend judgement till he had heard Maxfield. Wesley listened to Maxfield and was convinced. This meant a radical change in his preconceived ideas, but he accepted the advice of others and the verdict of experience. This is the more remarkable when we remember that Wesley was a man of increasingly autocratic tendencies. He lived to an advanced age and was active till the end; as the years passed his followers held him in increasing veneration, and his word was seldom challenged. This left a permanent imprint on the denomination which he unwittingly founded.

Wesley's influence has been described as "perhaps the most remarkable social phenomenon of the later eighteenth century."[14] Various attempts have been made to account for it. Wesley himself offered a very simple explanation. It was entirely due, he said, to the power of God fitting him for what he was called to do. He once made an illuminating comment about the work of A.H. Francke, the great Pietist leader in Germany. "So can God, if it pleaseth him, enable one man to revive his work throughout a whole nation."[15] The remark applies equally well to Wesley and his career. But it is permissible to examine the question in slightly greater detail. Wesley's phenomenal success was also due to a number of subsidiary considerations. He offered to others what he himself had found to be satisfying. He preached what had in his own case been confirmed by experience. His methods were adapted to the needs of the people whom he served. His mission was grounded in a theological system strong enough to bear the weight imposed upon it. The message he preached issued in a life marked by deep satisfaction and infectious joy. The change in his followers could be measured by the new spirit which permeated their societies. "I found them all alive, strong, vigorous of soul, blessing, loving, and praising God their Saviour....From the beginning they have been taught both the law and the gospel. 'God loves you; therefore love and obey him. Christ died for you: therefore die to sin. Christ is risen: therefore rise in the image of God. Christ liveth evermore: therefore live to God, till you live with him in glory.' So we preached, and so you believed. This is the Scriptural way, the Methodist way, the true way. God grant that we may never turn from it, to the right hand or to the left."[16]

One final quotation illustrates Wesley's strong emphasis on practical results. The lives of his followers were visibly and radically changed. "The drunkard commenced sober and temperate; the whoremonger abstained from adultery and fornication; the unjust from oppresssion and wrong. He that had been accustomed to curse and swear for many years, now swore no more. The sluggard began to work with his hands, that he might eat his own bread. The miser learned to deal his bread to the hungry, and to cover the naked with a garment. Indeed, the whole form of their life was changed. They left off doing evil, and learned to do well."[17]

Gerald R. Cragg

Notes

1. See J.D. Walsh, "Origins of the Evangelical Revival," in *Essays in Modern English Church History*, ed. G.V. Bennett and J.D. Walsh (London, 1966), pp. 138-48; see also J.D. Walsh, "Elie Halévy and the Birth of Methodism," in *Transactions of the Royal Historical Society*, 5th series, 25 (1975): 3.

2. Wesley, *Journal*, 18 Sept. to 5 Oct. 1745.

3. *Ibid.*, 27 May 1776.

4. *Ibid.*, letter of 10 Dec. 1734, printed in third instalment.

5. *Ibid.*, 28 May 1738.

6. Wesley, *A Farther Appeal to Men of Reason and Religion*, part 1, 1.27.

7. H. Walpole, letter to John Chute, 5 Oct. 1766.

8. Wesley, *Journal*, 27 Nov. 1750.

9. Wesley, *An Earnest Appeal to Men of Reason and Religion*, † 28.

10. *Ibid*, † 31.

11. Wesley, *A Farther Appeal*, part 3, IV.10.

12. Wesley, *Journal*, 2 Apr. 1739.

13. Wesley's headquarters in London; always so spelled.

14. A.R. Humphreys, *The Augustan Age* (London, 1954), p. 146.

15. Wesley, *Journal*, 20 Apr. 1748.

16. Wesley's description of the Yorkshire societies in 1751.

17. Wesley, *A Farther Appeal,* part 3, I.4.

The Sanctification of Nature

Following the Goodman-Hakewill controversy of the early seventeenth century there appeared in England a substantial body of writing which, in one way or another, declared the glory of God in the design of nature. George Hakewill himself had identified the central issue which divided him and Godfrey Goodman, noting that this controversy was grounded upon the interpretation of the phrase "cursed is the ground for thy sake" (Gen. 3:17). Hakewell had argued "That this curse extended to the changing of the principles of nature in the earth itself, we find not, much less that it reached unto the heavens."[1] In adopting this position he had rejected the apparently more orthodox tradition represented by Goodman. This tradition had been given authoritative statement during the Reformation by Calvin, who had said that we derive no benefit from the manifestation of God in His works,[2] and by Luther, who had interpreted Genesis 3:17 as applying to physical as well as to moral nature.[3] The doctrine of these theologians had come to be accepted generally as the orthodox Christian one, and so the views of Hakewill and his followers were seen as a major challenge to religious thought. The Goodman-Hakewill controversy was important because it focused attention upon the question of the reliability of nature as a source of evidence for the goodness, wisdom and power of God.

To determine just how far the curse did, or did not, extend into the realm of nature, men were exhorted to study physical nature in careful detail. The more careful the detail the better, because, as Thomas Sprat pointed out in his *History of the Royal Society*, the scientist would come to "admire the wonderful contrivance of the Creation, and so to apply and direct his praises aright, which no doubt, when they are offered up to heaven from the mouth of one who has well studied what he commends, will be more suitable in the Divine Nature than the blind applauses of the ignorant."[4] By the middle of the eighteenth century, acceptance of the evidence of nature had become widespread, and James Foster, for example, could talk with confidence about "a supreme all-creating Deity, whose footsteps and the evidence of his being, engraven in shining characters, may be distinctly traced through every part of the vast system of nature."[5] Mark Akenside, in his "Hymn to

Science," could take for granted the benefits which would result from a careful and informed examination of nature:

> Give me to learn each secret cause;
> Let number's, figure's, motion's, laws
> > Reveal'd before me stand;
> These to great Nature's scenes apply,
> And round the globe, and through the sky,
> > Disclose her working hand.[6]

Moses Browne, in *An Essay on the Universe*, exclaimed, "Nature! thy minutest Works amaze,/Poze the close Search and lose our Thoughts in Praise," and he urged man to "ponder Nature's Page,/There let clear Truth your pleas'd Assent engage;/And the dread God confess, his Sapience own,/Thro' the fill'd Space with brightest Lustre shown."[7] Over and over again during the eighteenth century, in both prose and verse, writers pondered the "brightest Lustre" of nature's design. The Boyle lectures were established for precisely this purpose.

At the conclusion of his Boyle lectures for 1711 and 1712, William Derham, after offering a survey of the "Works of Creation, or (as often called) of Nature," provided the following "practical inference" which echoes the argument of Sprat:

> The Creator doubtless did not bestow so much Curiosity, and exquisite Workmanship and Skill upon his Creatures, to be looked upon with a careless, incurious Eye, especially to have them slighted or condemned; but to be admired by the rational Part of the World, to magnify his own Power, Wisdom and Goodness, throughout all the World, and the Ages thereof. And therefore we may look upon it as a great Error not to answer those Ends of the infinite creator, but rather to oppose and affront them.[8]

These lectures draw our attention not only to the emerging confidence in mathematical description, but also to the continuing belief in the divine foundation of the universe. The purpose of the infinite creator was to "magnify his own Power, Wisdom and Goodness," and the achievements of the telescope and the microscope merely aided limited man in perceiving the extent of this magnification.

To disclose the working hand of nature the Royal Society devoted its considerable energies. A particularly clear rationale for this activity was provided by Joseph Glanvil in his *Philosophia Pia*. In the "Introduction" to this book he wrote: "It is the perverse opinion of hasty, inconsiderate Men, that the study of Nature is prejudicial to the interests of Religion; and those that are very zealous, and little wise, endeavour to render the Naturalist suspected of holding secret correspondence with the Atheist."[9] His own position — like that of his fellow members of the Royal Society — was articulated in what he called four "general heads" for his book:

> (1) That God is to be praised for His works.
>
> (2) That His works are to be studied by those that would praise Him for them.
>
> (3) That the study of Nature and God's works, is very serviceable to Religion.
>
> (4) That the Ministers and Professors of Religion ought not to discourage, but promote the knowledge of Nature and the Works of its Author.[10]

These principles, explained at length throughout the book, led to conclusions concerning the importance of this method for arriving at a full understanding of the impressive design created by God in nature:

> Hence I gather, that the study of God's works showing us more of the riches of nature, opens thereby a fairer prospect of those treasures of wisdom that are lodged within it; and so furnisheth us with deeper senses, and more arguments, and clearer convictions of the existence of an infinitely intelligent being, that contrived it in so harmonious, and astonishing an order.[11]

Nature, then, was proposed as an avenue for the apprehension of God and of the intended order of the universe.

How acceptable was this proposal is seen in the response during the 1680s to the publication of Thomas Burnet's *Sacred Theory of the Earth*, described by one modern scholar as "the conclusive statement of the idea of disorder.'' Michael Macklem has emphasized the importance of their response in defining and establishing the idea of order in the universe:

> The replies to Burnet's *Sacred Theory* rationalized the belief that the earth is not the natural estate of sin, a product of the curse and the Flood, but the work of divine providence, a product of the creation. Newton's theory of gravity extended this belief by showing that planetary motion requires both the original and the present agency of God. These conclusions, by emphasizing the identity of the original and present states of creation, made it possible to suppose that the curse did not alter the principles of nature, and that natural law is a description of the physical world as it is.[12]

The physical world as it is, then, became the sacred testament of God, *cosmologia sacra*, to borrow the title of the 1701 treatise by Nehemiah Grew. Grew himself was a member of the Royal Society, and it is significant to note how many of his colleagues were members of the clergy. The combination of professing Christian and enquiring scientist seemed to raise no difficulties at the time because both were ultimately concerned with the same subject matter: the wisdom, power and goodness of God. These divine attributes could be seen with increasing clarity and, consequently, accepted with increasing conviction, as man explored his universe with the aid of microscope and telescope. Robert Hooke opened the "Preface" to his influential *Micrographia* with the optimistic assertion: "It is the great prerogative of Mankind above other Creatures, that we are not only able to behold the works of Nature, or barely to sustain our lives by them, but we have also the power of considering, comparing, altering, assisting, and improving them to various uses."[13] To the theologians of the seventeenth and eighteenth centuries the primary use of the works of nature was to give evidence of divine design. The task of physics blended with that of theology, and physico-theological writings proliferated. The sacredness of nature became a major theme for scores of sermons, tracts, poems and treatises written throughout this period.

This attitude towards nature appears to be the product of a new interpretation of the passage in Genesis and of a new method for approaching the evidence. Gerald Cragg has said, "Gradually the balance shifted from what God has revealed to what man has discovered."[14] The order of nature took its place beside revelation as a valid and reliable source for evidence concerning the wisdom, power and goodness of God. Certainly, this was an enormously important development in the history of Western thought, and its influence — as we shall see later — was felt in virtually all realms of human activity. However, my first reaction is to wonder just how original or novel this development was felt to be at the time. I wonder if the physico-theologians viewed themselves as being in any way unorthodox, not to say revolutionary.

In his discussion of the physico-theological movement, particularly as it was expressed in the work of Burnet, Ray and Derham, Basil Willey — like most historians of scientific theory — has laid great stress on the element of originality. He wrote that "this view involved a changed attitude towards Nature and natural science; it meant that Nature was rescued from Satan and restored to God," and went on to explain exactly what he meant by this rescue operation by a summary of the historical development in scientific theory as he viewed it:

> For the physical world, in spite of its divine origin, was traditionally held to have shared in the fatal consequences of the fall of man, and to have become the chosen abode of the apostate spirits. Science in the Middle Ages was largely black magic; Nature was full of pagan divinities turned devils, and to meddle with it was to risk damnation. Friar Bacon was imprisoned as a sorcerer, and the Faust story illustrates the fascinated horror with which, as late as the sixteenth century, the popular mind regarded scientific knowledge. But now the more fortunate Francis Bacon could announce with conviction and authority that science was not the forbidden knowledge; that God has provided two channels of revelation, not one merely: the Scriptures, of course, but Nature also.[15]

In general outline this is a fair enough indication of the way in which attitudes towards scientific experimentation and discovery evolved over the centuries. Certainly it is an accurate summary of the physico-theologians' attitude towards nature. But we must ask, did not man always have access to God's revelation through the design of nature? Laymen, as well as theologians, were thoroughly familiar with the many biblical passages — especially in the Psalms — which emphasized the divinity of nature. The introduction to Robert Wallace's "Prospect V" was a masterful compendium of this material.[16] The many translations and paraphrases of the Psalms throughout the eighteenth century testify to the hold which this material had upon the popular imagination as well as upon the religious thought of the age. The intention of this paper is to examine how the physico-theological writers responded to these biblical passages and how they related to traditions of Christian thought other than the more orthodox one represented by Goodman.

Not all traditions of Christian thought emphasized the fatal consequences of the fall of man, nor did they all see nature as having shared this lapse. Half a century before, John Ray had declared that the wisdom of God is manifested in the works of creation. John Smith had said the same thing:

> God made the universe and all the creatures contained therein as so many glasses wherein he might reflect his own glory. He hath copied forth himself in the creation; and in this outward world we may read the lovely characters of Divine goodness, power, and wisdom.[17]

Like other Cambridge Platonists, Smith sought knowledge of the Lord not from logical argument, but through an inner state of wisdom which unites truth and goodness: "That which enables us to know and understand aright in the things of God, must be a living principle of Holiness within us."[18] Smith's tutor while he was at Emmanuel College, Cambridge, Benjamin Whichcote, wrote: "This is a very profitable work to call upon men, to answer the principles of their creation, to fulfil natural light, to answer natural conscience, to be throughout rational in what they do; for these things have a Divine foundation.[19] Of the work by the Cambridge Platonists generally, it can be said what has been said of Cudworth's "Sermon before the House of Commons": it "touches nearly all the most difficult theological problems — the nature of God, sin, atonement, justification, sanctification, salvation — and brings them all into relation with the life of love."[20] These writers addressed themselves to the usual topics of Christian theology but tended to discuss them within a special context.

These exhortations by the physico-theologians and by the Cambridge Platonists are, I suggest, particularly meaningful if they are understood not as expressions of a revolutionary and secularized approach to the created universe, but as part of an ancient and continuous concept of the sanctification of nature. Man himself and the whole physical world give evidence of the "wonderful contrivance of the creator" and there is a "living principle of Holiness within us," for "these things have a Divine foundation." These writers chose to explore and to emphasize the divinity in that foundation, rather than to enumerate and lament the number of cracks which had appeared since the fall and the deluge. Their concern was with nature as it relates to the sequence of creation, redemption and sanctification. Their reasoning was similar to that put forward by a modern theologian: "If God is God, and God is manifested in Christ, then Creation, Redemption and Sanctification must be identical in origin and fundamentally also in character."[21]

In propounding his doctrine of salvation John Wesley gave a convenient sketch of the meaning of sanctification by relating it to justification:

> [Justification] is not the being made actually just and righteous. This is sanctification; which is, indeed, in some degree, the immediate fruit of justification, but, nevertheless, is a distant gift of God, and of a totally different nature. The one implies, what God does for us through His Son; the other, what He works in us by His spirit.[22]

A modern commentator has elaborated upon these concepts:

> Yet from the moment of justification sanctification itself set in, the more or less gradual acquisition of holiness, "the image of God" — "the mind that was in Christ" — and "stamped," Wesley said, upon the heart and brain of either collier or gentleman (the Christian and the psychologist in Wesley made no distinction between them). Sanctification, there, in

> spite of man's necessary ignorance, infirmities, and liability to temptation, was perfection.[23]

Sanctification, in spite of man's frailties and limitations, is a state as close to perfection as the human condition will allow. But this state can be extended beyond man in isolation to the universe in which man finds himself and (perhaps most important) to the relationship between man and that universe. The exhortations of the Cambridge Platonists, like those of the early Church Fathers, were delivered within the context of such a harmony. Nature, to them, was sanctified — that is, a special creation by God, still bearing the means of grace. Nature has a "divine foundation."

It is this "divine foundation" which I believe the physico-theologians were trying to rediscover. They were using the convenient tools of scientific observation to reassert, in the face of considerable popular opposition (as their insistent self-explanation indicates), a concept of nature which is the mirror of the Almighty. They were, I believe, asserting the sanctification of nature, although I am unaware that any of them ever actually put it in these terms.

However, to assert the sanctification of nature was to come face to face with a peculiar theological difficulty. The context for the discussion of sanctification, especially since the high Middle Ages, had been focused upon man and his need for redemption. Derived in part from St. Augustine's books written against Pelagius and Coelestius, and reinforced by the teachings of Calvin and Luther, it emphasized man's disobedience and fall rather than any original intention evident in creation. There was a tendency to identify man with his depravity, rather than with a continuing relationship in grace between man and nature. In other words, grace came to be seen as discontinuous and antithetical to nature. The inevitable conclusion to this line of thought was a rejection of the concept that nature was the icon of divine being and that the attributes of God could be clearly seen in the operation of nature. Nature was viewed as man's great enemy, rather than as *cosmologia sacra*. The original harmonic relationship had been gravely disrupted. This is the attitude found in a number of works composed during the late seventeenth and the eighteenth centuries, including Bunyan's *Grace Abounding*, John Edwards' *Theologia Reformata*, Thomas Bowman's *Principles of Christianity* and Thomas Scott's *A Treatise on Growth in Grace*. It was given poetic expression in many of the hymns by Wesley and by Cowper.

To restore the original harmony between man and the divine requires an act of grace, or sanctification. Traditionally there have been two emphases in the doctrine of sanctification: Calvin puts it on the action of God continually renewed, and the Roman Catholics on the results, in man, of God's act. (The Eastern Orthodox Church has tended to express views on this subject similar to those of the Roman Catholic Church). But however varied may be the means and the extent, the possibility of sanctification has always existed in Christian theology, and in some quarters this possibility has been closely allied with nature.

It is not surprising, therefore, to find Richard Hooker concluding the first book of his *Of the Laws of Ecclesiastical Polity* with the following summary:

> ...of Law there can be no less acknowledged, than that her seat is the bosom of God, her voice the harmony of the world: all things in heaven and earth do her homage, the very least as feeling her care, and the greatest as not exempted from her power.[24]

The doctrine of Hooker was similar to that articulated later by the Cambridge Platonists, of whom a modern scholar has said: "Nature and the natural order are to them not only God's creation but the foundation of true religion both moral and philosophical; there is nothing incongruous, indeed nothing contradictory between nature and grace."[25] Indeed, it was upon these grounds that Anthony Tuckney based his strong objections to Whichcote. Archbishop Tillotson aligned himself with Whichcote when he wrote about "nothing being more incredible, than that Divine Revelation should contradict the clear and unquestionable Dictates of Natural Light; nor any thing more vain, than to fancy that the Grace of God does release Men from the Laws of Nature."[26] There seems, therefore, to have been a significant tradition within the Anglican Church which recognized value in natural light and the laws of nature. On the matter of natural reason it has been pointed out that Daniel Waterland appealed to the authority of "a lengthy catena of medieval and post-Tridentine scholastics" and therefore apparently recognized "a continuous tradition from St. Thomas Aquinas to his own day, including the most famous of the latitude-men."[27] This continuous tradition did not presume to extol revolutionary or eccentric doctrines of Christianity, but merely to talk about orthodox concerns within a context different from that used by the Calvinists.

It is not inappropriate, therefore, to find in the eighteenth century two traditions of theological thought which existed side-by-side. These have been distinguished as "Redemptionist" and "Incarnationist," and it is possible to identify them by their views of grace.[28] Indeed, the Incarnationist tradition has been described as "one which from Hooker onward has been the peculiar possession and characteristic of the Anglican communion, distinguishing Anglican theology rather sharply from that traditional in the Lutheran and Reformed churches."[29] The importance of this Incarnationist tradition for our study is that it be recognized as a significant element in eighteenth-century Christian thought and that it be seen as a means for reconciling nature and grace. This latter point was stated most unambiguously by Bishop Berkeley:

> It will be sufficient, if such analogy appears between the dispensations of grace and nature, as may make it probable (although much should be unaccountable in both) to suppose them derived from the same Author, and the workmanship of one and the same Hand.[30]

Here, in essence, is the approach and the method which we have noted among the physico-theological writers.

When the viability of resolution between nature and grace has been recognized, certain topics come to be stressed more frequently. Four of these will attract our attention briefly in this study: harmony, vindication, providence, and variety.

Thomas Browne's *Garden of Cyrus* was a particularly eloquent vision of the harmony of the sacred cosmos, where "all things began in order, so shall they end, and so shall they begin again, according to the ordainer of order and mystical mathematics of the City of Heaven."[31] But it was only one work in a very large number which were concerned with the harmony of the universe. Of these, John Gilbert Cooper's *The Power of Harmony* was the most thorough statement of the importance of harmony to the perception of divine perfection and beauty. He described his purpose in this poem as "to show that a constant attention to what is perfect and beautiful in nature will by degrees harmonize the soul to a responsive regularity and sympathetic order."[32] This intention occupied the time and efforts of scores of physico-theologians who wanted to trace the beauty and harmony of the created world as evidence of the creative focus behind it, for, as Isaac Newton reasoned, "this most beautiful System of the Sun, Planets, and Comets, could only proceed from the counsel and dominion of an intelligent and powerful Being."[33]

In carrying out this intention they were concerned with vindicating the ways of God to man. It is significant that they chose the verb "to vindicate," rather than the more Calvinist one "to justify" chosen by Milton. It is also interesting that in *Paradise Lost* Milton stressed that at the eating of the apple, first by Eve and then by Adam:

> Earth felt the wound, and Nature from her seat,
> Sighing through all her works, gave signs of woe
> That all was lost.[34]

However, when John Hopkins elected to imitate the ninth book of *Paradise Lost* in rhyming couples, he omitted all allusions to the fall of nature. Whereas Milton was concerned to "assert Eternal Providence,/And justify the ways of God to men"[35] within the tradition of redemptionist theology the physico-theologians saw, with John Ogilvie, a "Paradise restored"[36] and attempted to explain their vision in terms of the Incarnation and the end for which all things were created. Thus the provenance of nature could be taken as reliable evidence. The poet-laureate Henry James Pye, in 1774, suggested that this had already been done:

> These scenes could Addison's chaste notes inspire,
> Here Pope harmonious struck his silver lyre,
> Caught 'midst these solemn shades the glorious plan,
> "To vindicate the ways of God to man."[37]

As late as 1781 the Reverend Joseph Wise believed it necessary to respond to sceptical adversaries who questioned the meaning of evil in the universe and who challenged him:

> Resolve these queries wisely, if you can,
> And vindicate the ways of God to man.

In resolving the problem of evil, Wise arrived at a conclusion which is identical to that propounded by Pope in *An Essay on Man* (which also sets as its goal to "vindicate the ways of God to Man"), but Wise stated his conclusion within a different context of evidence:

> Behold, his Glory stands the final View!
> The universe to glorify him grew.
> What'er emerges from created pow'r,
> Evil or good, it glorifies him more.
> Wisdom, pow'r, freedom, in each work we trace;
> More they expand with equity and grace:
> In holiness sublime mature they meet:
> His glory there shines aggrandiz'd complete.
> Thus all his attributes, divinely bright,
> Fully display'd. Whatever is, is right![38]

The vindication of God's ways for the physico-theologians took the form of recognizing the design of Providence in nature. Samuel Pratt pleaded, "O! thou proud Christian, aid fair nature's grace."[39] And in the "Introduction" to his long poem *Providence*, John Ogilvie summed up the purpose and the method of this tradition of soteriology:

> The complete vindication of the ways of God to man, we must leave to that day, in which the secrets of the heart will be laid open, and the Deity's moral government of the world, as it regards the circumstances of individuals, will be justified in the presence of its assembled inhabitants. It is sufficient with our limited and scanty portion of knowledge, if from considering things as they are at present, we can account for some of the dispensations of Providence, in such a manner as may convince us that the marks of design which reflection suggests to us, point to some Being of superior wisdom who is employed to regulate the revolution of events.[40]

The same purpose and method had been applied almost a quarter of a century earlier by George Turnbull to the principles of moral philosophy. His rubric to Part 1 announced: "Human Nature and the ways of God to man vindicated, by delineating the general laws to which the principle phenomena in the human system are reducible, and showing them to be wise and good."[41]

These quotations indicate the enormous importance attached by certain writers of the eighteenth century to the vindication of God's ways; they were consciously responding to the work of Milton, but they believed that the assertion of eternal Providence should be carried out within the context of a nature to which grace had been restored.

In saying that "we can account for some of the dispensations of Providence" by "considering things as they are at present," Ogilvie was taking for granted certain aspects concerning the sphere and operation of divine law. One modern historian of the scientific movement has argued that during the eighteenth century there was a change from a concept of specific to general providence.[42] While this change had many implications, it is important to note that the role of God as sustainer of the operation of the universe continued to be stressed:

> If men of the 18th century looked upon the world as an autonomous machine, the Christian virtuosi affirmed that divine sustenance is necessary to its operation. Their final idea of general providence, painfully worked out by a number of thinkers, was more than a rejoicing of the doctrine of particular providence. In asserting the primacy of spiritual control, it was a true reconciliation between science and religion.[43]

This true reconciliation is what Ogilvie assumed in his long poem *Providence*. God was understood to be both creator and sustainer of the universe. His providence presupposed continued care for his creation. Other writers expressed similar views. Thus William Roberts took pains to refute those who took too literally the analogy of the universe as a machine and, therefore, concluded that in some way it could run itself. He reminded his readers of the continuous care of the creator: "His hand supports/The golden chain, that links a thousand worlds."[44] Like many other physico-theological writers he made a point of rejecting any doctrine which implied either (with Aristotle) the eternity of the universe or (with Lucretius) its creation and operation by

98

chance. God's involvement with the universe is a major theme of Roberts' poem:

> . . . the expanse of heaven God's praise proclaims,
> The firmament his power: day tells to day,
> And night to night, his providential care.

A fuller assertion of God's sustaining power occurred in Henry Baker's poem *The Universe*:

> 'Tis He alone sustains this Orb in Air,
> His Creatures breathe by his paternal Care:
> His Goodness does their daily Food supply,
> And if he but withholds his Hand, they die,
> 'Tis He within due Bounds the Floods restrains:
> He swells the Brooks which murmur O'er the Plains,
> And from the Mountains pours the seasonable Rains.
> He gives the Word: the blust'ring Winds arise:
> On Billows Billows mounted storm the Skies.[45]

Abraham Portal wrote of the continuous love of God for his creation:

> Nor does here
> Thy wound'rous Love desist; but, rolling on
> Thro' Ages infinite, with Providence
> Unerring still preserves the glorious Works
> Which thy right Hand hath made.[46]

These sentiments presuppose a view of nature as sanctified. It was the view which the physico-theologians had been diligently seeking to establish. God was both creator and sustainer of the universe. His providence included the creative act of sustenance.

Variety, then, became an aspect of providential care. Thomson's *The Seasons* is a familiar illustration of this concern, especially the hymn which concludes the series of poems;

> These, as they change, Almighty Father! these
> Are but the varied God. The rolling year
> Is full of thee.[47]

Here, as in many works of the period, the diversity of natural phenomena is taken to be evidence of the wide-ranging creative power and completeness of God. As one modern critic has put it: "The seasons represent a form of divine order; they are thoroughly appropriate as a structure for glorifying God through His works — and the glorification of God is perhaps the primary motive for *The Seasons.*"[48] This was certainly the primary motive for the large body of physico-theological writing during the late seventeenth and the eighteenth centuries. They asserted providence in the design of the universe, and the proving of this design gave evidence of the wisdom, power, and goodness of God. In full cognizance of the implications of what he was writing, Edward Young could suggest that we might call the firmament "The Garden of the Deity."[49]

These doctrines concerning harmony, vindication, providence and variety were not heretical, let alone revolutionary, doctrines. The physico-theologians were devoted to articulating orthodox views, but they expressed them within a context that varied from the tradition of Augustine and Luther. Their central concept was the sanctification of nature, and this concept was an enormously important one, not only for the writers of sermons and tracts, but also for the poets of what I call the physico-theological epics. By this genre I mean such works as Sir Richard Blackmore's *The Creation*, Robert Gambol's *The Beauties of the Universe*, Henry Brooke's *Universal Beauty* and William Willis's *The Sacrifice*, as well as those poems from which I have quoted in this essay. These writings were sufficiently influential throughout the century to establish that the concepts with which they were concerned were relevant and meaningful to a wide range of the reading public.

The concept of the sanctification of nature was potentially an enormously popular one, for, once it was established, it could appear to give sanction in a great number of fields. The most popular, of course, was morality, where it was argued that there was, as John Gilbert Cooper succinctly put it, an "analogy between natural and moral beauty."[50] Thus nature became moralized.[51]

But the implications of the concept spread to other areas, until society, reason, imagination, benevolence, justice and all forms of order were seen to be dependent upon it. Indeed, the importance of this concept was summed up by Samuel Clarke in his Boyle lectures for 1705:

> Without this, All comes to Nothing: If this Scheme
> be once broken; there is no justice, no Goodness, no
> Order, no Reason, nor any thing upon which any
> Argument in moral matters can be founded, left in
> the World.[52]

The concept of the sanctification of nature, which informed the writings of the physico-theologians and of the poets of physico-theological epics, was a concept of enormous importance to the later seventeenth and the eighteenth centuries. It traced its origin from writings of the early church fathers and expressed an attitude concerning grace which was similar to that found in traditions of the Eastern Orthodox and Roman Catholic churches. The physico-theologians saw no problem in applying scientific investigation to nature because they conceived it as still retaining evidence of God as wisdom, power and goodness.[53] In writing as they did about nature, they did not so much introduce a new concept of nature or a new method of studying it, as substitute a different context for describing it. Their work, as they conceived it, like the subject matter of their study, had a "divine foundation."

Grant Sampson

Notes

1. George Hakewill, *Apologie; or Declaration of the Power and Providence of God in the Government of the World, 1627*, (1635), p. 56. See Victor Harris, *All Coherence Gone* (Chicago, 1949), chap. 3. Marjorie Nicolson, *Mountain Gloom and Mountain Glory* (Ithaca, 1959), pp. 105–110; Michael Macklem, *The Anatomy of the World* (Minneapolis, 1958), chap. 2. Godfrey Goodman's *The Fall of Man; or, The Corruption of Nature, Proved by the Light of our Natural Reason* had been published in 1616.

2. Jean Calvin, *Institutes*, trans. Henry Beveridge (Edinburgh, 1879), 5:59.

3. Martin Luther, *Works*, ed. Jaroslov Pelikan (St. Louis, 1958), 1:204.

4. Thomas Sprat, *The History of the Royal Society of London for the Improving of Natural Knowledge* (London, 1667), p. 349.

5. James Foster, *Discourses on All the Principal Branches of Natural Religion and Social Virtue* (London, 1749), 1:21.

6. Mark Akenside, "Hymn to Science," *Poetical Works* ed. G. Gilfillan (Edinburgh, 1857) p. 291.

7. Moses Browne, *Poems on Various Subjects* (London, 1739), pp. 300, 384-85.

8. William Derham, *Physico-theology; or, A Demonstration of the Being and Attributes of God, from His Works of Creation* (London, 1727), 3:427.

9. Joseph Glanvil, *Philosophia Pia; or, A Discourse of the Religious Temper, and Tendencies of the Experimental Philosophy, Which is Profest by the Royal Society* (London, 1671), p. 1.

10. *Ibid.,* p. 4.

11. *Ibid.,* p. 19.

12. Macklem, pp. 25, 92.

13. Robert Hooke, *Micrographia, or some Physiological Descriptions of Minute Bodies made by Magnifying glasses* (London, 1665), "Preface."

14. Gerald R. Cragg, *The Church and the Age of Reason (1648-1789)* (Harmondsworth, 1960), p. 13. For his interpretation of the relation between science and religion, see *From Puritanism to the Age of Reason* (Cambridge, 1950), p. 229.

15. Basil Willey, *The Eighteenth Century Background* (London, 1940), p. 4. See also, Ian G. Barbour, *Issues in Science and Religion* (New York, 1971), pp. 23-69.

16. Robert Wallace, *Various Prospects of Mankind, Nature, and Providence* (London, 1761), pp. 129-30.

17. Quoted in Cragg, *The Church*, p. 69.

18. Quoted in Paul Elmer More and Frank Leslie Cross, eds., *Anglicanism* (London, 1957), pp. 223-40.

19. *Ibid.,* p. 213.

20. Geoffrey P.H. Pawson, *The Cambridge Platonists and their Place in Religious Thought* (London, 1930), pp. 72-73.

21. Charles Raven, *Natural Religion and Christian Theology* (Cambridge, 1953), 1:3.

22. John Wesley, *Standard Sermons*, ed. E.H. Sugden, (London, 1961), 1:119.

23. Lewis P. Curtis, *Anglican Moods of the Eighteenth Century* (Hamden, Conn., 1966), p. 73.

24. Richard Hooker, *Of the Laws of Ecclesiastical Polity* (London: Dent, 1958), 1:232.

25. Raven, *Natural Religion*, 1:111.

26. John Tillotson, "Preface" to John Wilkins, *Of the Principles and Duties of Natural Religion* (London, 1678), no page.

27. Samuel L. Bethell, *The Cultural Revolution of the Seventeenth Century* (London, 1951), p. 18.

28. See Philip S. Watson, *The Concept of Grace* (Philadelphia, 1959), pp. 77-83; Joseph Sittler, *Essays on Nature and Grace* (Philadelphia, 1972), pp. 73-91; C. Moeller and G. Philips, *The Theology of Grace* (London, 1961), pp. 46-48; William Temple, *Nature, Man and God* (London, 1934), passim; and a critical response, Leonard Hodgon, *The Grace of God in Faith and Philosophy* (London, 1936), passim.

29. Julian V. Langmead Casserley, *Graceful Reason: The Contribution of Reason to Theology* (Greenwich, 1954) p. 129.

30. George Berkeley, "Alciphon," in *Works*, ed. A.A. Luce and T.E.E Jessop, (London, 1950), 3:281.

31. Sir Thomas Browne, *The Works*, ed. Geoffrey Keynes (London, 1928), 4:125.

32. John Gilbert Cooper, "The Power of Harmony," in *Minor English Poets 1660-1780*, ed. David P. French (New York, 1967), 5: 365.

33. Quoted in More and Cross, *Anglicanism*, p. 230.

34. John Milton, *Paradise Lost* 9: 782-84; see also 9:1000-1004.

35. *Ibid*. 25-26.

36. John Ogilvie, *Paradise* (London, 1769), line 28.

37. Henry James Pye, *Faringdon Hill* (Oxford, 1774), p. 20.

38. Joseph Wise, *The System,* (London, 1781), 8:26-27.

39. Samuel Pratt, *Humanity* (London, 1788), p. 41.

40. John Ogilvie, *Providence* (London, 1764), pp. xii-xiii.

41. George Turnbull, *The Principles of Moral Philosophy* (London, 1740), Part I.

42. Richard S. Westfall, *Science and Religion in Seventeenth-Century England* (New Haven, 1958), Ch. IV.

43. *Ibid*., 105.

44. William Roberts, *A Poetical Essay on the Existence of God* (London, 1771), Part II, 5; Part III, 10-11.

45. Henry Baker, *The Universe* (London, 1727) 20.

46. Abraham Portal, *Innocence* (London, 1762) 80, 82.

47. James Thomson, *The Seasons,* "A Hymn," lines 1-3.

48. Patricia Spacks, *The Varied God* (Berkeley, 1959), 22.

49. Edward Young, *Night Thoughts* (London, 1747), 267.

50. John Gilbert Cooper. "The Power of Harmony," in *Minor English Poets 1660-1780,* ed., David P. French (New York, 1967), V. 369.

51. See Earl R. Wasserman, *"Natural Moralized: The Divine Analogy in the Eighteenth Century," ELH,* XX (1953), 39-76.

52. Samuel Clarke, *A Discourse Concerning the Unchangeable Obligations of Natural Religion* (London, 1706), 174-75.

53. See Stephen Neill, *Anglicanism* (Harmondsworth, 1958), 171; and Norman Sykes, *The English Religious Tradtion* (London, 1961), 53.

A Social Contract: the Poor, the Privileged and the Church in Eighteenth-Century Spain

Between 1835 and 1841 the Spanish Church of the old regime, with its enormous wealth, its numerous and colourful religious orders, its archaic and imbalanced administrative structure and its elaborate Baroque ceremonial, disappeared before the onslaught of the triumphant Spanish liberalism that had taken power after the death of the absolutist Ferdinand VII in 1833. The key to the liberal attack on the Church, a series of disentailing laws directed at first at the property of monasteries and convents and later at that of the secular clergy, dramatically altered the role which the Church had played for centuries within Spanish society.[1] Without the revenues provided by real estate and tithes, the Baroque Church could no longer sustain the grandiose ecclesiastical super-structure that had been built between the sixteenth and eighteenth centuries. The sale of monastic property destroyed most of the religious orders, the loss of episcopal and diocesan property quickly reduced the social status and economic significance of the secular clergy, or at least those portions of it controlling ecclesi-astical wealth and government, and more importantly, the Church lost the means of financing the myriad of charitable and educa-tional activities which had made it an institution touching the lives of all social classes.

The collapse of clerical finances as a result of disentailment led to the disintegration of ecclesiastical charity and the transfer of responsibility for social welfare to the state and private philan-thropy. By 1840, supporters of the Church were lamenting the decline of religious charity, that "fruitful Christian charity" as one author expressed it, contrasting with "sterile philanthropy."[2] The distinction between charity and philanthropy so frequently cited by commentators of the 1830s and 1840s reflected funda-mentally different approaches to the problem of poor relief, differences between a system demanding help for the impoverished as an essential aspect of the quest for salvation and one analyzing the problem in purely secular and pragmatic terms. The shift from charity to philanthropy represented a radical departure from the way Spanish society had long dealt with the poor.

The problem itself was massive. Eighteenth-century visitors to the kingdom were constantly startled by the crowds of impoverished begging in city streets and before churches and convents. The archbishop of Granada in the 1780s counted on one occasion more than 5,000 paupers waiting at his palace gates for the daily distribution of alms, while an English visitor to the Peninsula during the same period complained of the "multitude of beggars, infesting every street in Málaga," and the swarms of mendicants roaming Alicante in search of alms.[3] Nor was the countryside exempt. Bands of roving beggars wandered through the rural districts of Catalonia and Salamanca during the late eighteenth century, occasionally terrorizing local residents with their insistent pleas for help. The poor, then, were present everywhere in eighteenth-century Spain, and their presence was an accepted fact of urban and rural social life.

If the problem was massive, the response was equally so. The Church, through the episcopacy, cathedral chapters, monasteries and convents and religious associations formed for charitable purposes, dispensed the alms, food and clothing which often meant the difference between survival and death for the indigent. This is not to idealize the efficiency of a poor relief system dependent upon the Church. Charity was often haphazardly and undependably distributed; it did not seek to resolve the deep economic causes of poverty in a pre-industrial economy. And it should be kept in mind that the Spanish Church of the eighteenth century possessed the immense financial resources necessary to provide assistance for the poor and that it did not impoverish itself in doing so. We do not have overall figures to indicate how much of its wealth the Church committed to charity, largely because of the fragmented nature of ecclesiastical poor relief. There is, however, evidence indicating that individual churchmen and clerical institutions set aside a considerable portion of their income on the poor, and an eighteenth-century account of the archbishop of Granada tells us:

> His bounty to the poor is such, that we can scarcely
> conceive his income to equal his expenditure. Beside
> private pensions to families and occasional relief in
> seasons of distress, he provides nurses in the country
> for 440 orphans and deserted children; he sends poor

patients to the hot baths at the distance of eight leagues from Granada, where he actually maintains fourscore, and he daily distributes bread to all the poor, who assemble at his door...In this bounty he is imitated by forty convents at which are distributed bread and broth without discrimination to all who present themselves.[4]

Monasteries and convents distributed alms as a matter of course, and perhaps no scene was more familiar to eighteenth-century Spaniards than the crowds of paupers gathered outside the gates of religious houses awaiting the daily distribution of food.

The charitable example of the Church was imitated by numerous voluntary associations (*hermandades*, *cofradías*, *congregaciones*) actively engaged in poor relief in the towns. Although such groups came into being for religious motives, the performance of good works in the pursuit of a spiritual goal, they contributed significantly to urban charitable efforts, approximating in primitive fashion the social agencies of the modern city. In Madrid, for example, the brotherhood of San Fernando gathered mendicants from the streets and furnished them food and lodging; the congregation of San Felipe Neri sent its members to work in the city's charity hospitals; the brotherhood of the Refugio maintained an active programme of charity which assisted an average of 5,000 persons a year during the eighteenth century; the congregation of Santísimo Cristo de Consuelo buried paupers who had died without means.[5] These charitable associations provided the vehicle for extensive noble participation in urban poor relief. Not all charitable groups were noble in social composition, but in general the nobility dominated the world of private charity.[6] The brotherhood of the Refugio in Madrid included grandees of Spain, as well as many noblemen of lesser rank, and its pattern of membership was similar to that of similar associations in the capital. Through the charitable associations the privileged were able to fulfill the obligation of charity demanded by the Church.

There persisted in Spain throughout the eighteenth century a system of poor relief that was primarily religious in purpose. Spain lagged far behind the initiatives taken elsewhere, even in Catholic Europe, to place poor relief on a more organized and indirectly secular basis. Sixteenth-century Venice, for example, had developed a highly bureaucratic scheme of public assistance which, though ostensibly moved by religious considerations, was in fact a system of charity regulated by the state to provide relief on the basis of need, in place of the chaotic and often indiscriminate distribution of alms by the Church, pious foundations and individuals. And in the France of Louis XIV, the state acted vigorously to deal with the problem of the poor through an openly repressive policy of incarcerating paupers without regular means of employment. But in Spain, it was not until the reign of Charles III (1759–1788) that the state began to intervene actively in the field of social welfare. Only then did it create a series of municipal charity boards (*juntas de caridad*), such as those established in some European cities during the sixteenth century, and promote the establishment of poorhouses (*hospicios*) to contain mendicants cleared from the streets by police action. The success of these measures was limited, however, and did not alter the basic structure of a poor relief system resting heavily on the charitable efforts of the Church and the nobility. Until the end of the old regime, charity inspired by religious motives formed the basis of Spanish society's response to the problem of poverty.

The persistence in Spain of a religiously motivated system of social welfare until well into the nineteenth century had many causes, some of them practical. The chronic fiscal difficulties of the state through the seventeenth and early eighteenth centuries prevented the adoption of the costly French system of poorhouses. Even when such institutions appeared after 1750, many failed because of inadequate financing. Moreover, within the social and economic context of the eighteenth century, the system of religious charity worked reasonably well and certainly more effectively than the poorhouses and municipal charity boards created by Charles III. In times of severe economic crisis and food shortages, religious charity was capable of mobilizing resources far more effectively than the state. When a terrible winter in 1768-69 destroyed crops in Galicia and thousands of starving peasants filled Santiago de Compostela, it was not the government but the church — the archbishop, the cathedral chapter and the monasteries of the city — who fed them and organized a relief campaign which would do credit to modern social agencies as thousands of *reales* were raised to purchase grain supplies in southern France.[7] Although the state became increasingly concerned with the Church's tendency to provide help indiscriminately to anyone who asked, irrespective of need, in the final analysis government authorities were unwilling to tamper with a system of poor relief which, if it did not resolve the problem of poverty, at least mitigated its worst disasters.

There is, I believe, a deeper reason to account for the survival of an extensive and relatively effective system of charity dominated by the nobility and the Church. Although the Catholic interpretation of the place of poverty in the grand providential design for mankind and the scholastic analysis of the nature and purposes of human society, both with their intellectual origins in the Middle Ages, still formed the official ideology of Catholic Europe, the gap between social reality and traditional theological and philosophical thought was becoming more and more obvious elsewhere. But in Spain, there is evidence that the privileged classes continued to accept a corporate, collective view of society in which each social class formed part of a community in which each class laboured under obligations towards the others. This was not, of course, a social contract in the sense of Rousseau, but it was a contract which had meaning within the confines of a traditional hierarchical society. It was also a contract in that its terms were known and understood by rich and poor alike.

The Church itself saw to it that knowledge of the terms of the contract was widely diffused. A survey of the leading eighteenth-century collections of sermons reveals the extraordinary importance preachers of the time attached to the theme of poverty and the necessity of charity, for few topics were more extensively or frequently discussed.[8] Anyone attending services with regularity, even the illiterate, would inevitably hear a sermon or homily on charity, and such discussions were often very detailed, given the propensity of eighteenth-century preachers for long sermons. The educated public was even more exposed to the Church's exhortations to charity. The only authentic best sellers of the eighteenth century, the biographies of the saints and prominent religious figures and the innumerable guides for spiritual and moral direction of the faithful published by ecclesiastics, constantly extolled the importance of charity in a well-ordered Christian society. Perhaps the most popular spiritual guide of the eighteenth century, Antonio Arbiol's *La familia regulada*, which appeared in at least seven editions, devoted an entire chapter to charity, and similar works did likewise.[9] Library inventories of the period reveal that few homes lacked copies of at least several of these works.[10] Few among rich and poor could have been unaware of the Church's teaching on the question of poverty and charity.

The doctrine of charity espoused by the eighteenth-century Church rested on its interpretation of the enormous disparities of wealth clearly evident to all. How could one account for the riches of the few and the grinding poverty of the many? According to Francisco Bocanegra, the archbishop of Santiago during the 1770s, it was not chance, hard work or the good fortune of one's ancestors that made some wealthy and others poor, but God himself: "The intention of God in making some men rich is to make them charitable; those chosen to enjoy this grace do so because they have been made instruments of divine mercy."[11] The idea that men were given worldly goods to help the poor was tied, in turn, to a concept of property held in absolute terms by individuals to dispose of as they liked. Poverty was bestowed on man, according to the celebrated Jesuit preacher, Pedro de Calatayud, as a trust held under the condition of aiding the poor: "The rich...were created and constituted by God, as administrators and majordomos of property so that they might distribute it to the poor."[12]

Clerics also extolled the spiritual benefits accruing to those practising charity, especially those endowed with an abundance of worldly goods. The Church still tenaciously held to the idea that the rich faced temptations making their salvation difficult. An eighteenth- century catechism posed the question: "Is it a sin to be rich?" and gave the reply: "No, although it is very difficult for the rich man not to live in sin."[13] To overcome the spiritual dangers facing the well-to-do, charity was necessary, for, according to Pedro de Calatayud, it was "a lawyer standing before the tribunal of God seeking to persuade him to dictate a favourable sentence."[14]

Clerical exhortations to the rich were more than vague appeals for good works. Churchmen made it abundantly clear, sometimes in harsh language, that charity was an obligation which the wealthy must fulfill if they hoped to be saved. "To distribute alms," said Pedro de Calatayud, "is not advice, it is a natural and divine law which binds under pain of mortal sin."[15] For Archbishop Bocanegra, alms-giving was a "rigourous obligation imposed by the law," and the individuals failing to practise it, "men without mercy or piety who will be cast into the eternal fire, the most just and inevitable punishment for their offence."[16] Cardinal Lorenzana of Toledo, using legal language familiar to the Spanish nobility, compared the obligation of charity to a kind of *censo*, a loan of capital provided in this case by God to the rich on condition that the interest due the lender be paid to the poor.[17]

If the privileged were left in no doubt about the necessity of charity on their part, the poor were equally aware that they had not merely a claim to the generosity of their betters but a right to it. Pedro de Calatayud publicly declared that the state should compel "the avaricious rich" to give alms "because the good of the people takes precedence over the gains and comforts of the rich."[18] Bocanegra held that the impoverished deserved assistance because the doctrines of the Church demanded it and because they had "a great right" to it according to the laws of humanity.[19] Moreover, poverty was not regarded as an evil in itself, a human condition meriting the punishment and condemnation of society. In a sense, the Church's theology of charity was democratic, for differences of wealth and social status would mean nothing in the hereafter.[20] Archbishop Rodríguez Arellano of Burgos attacked those believing that the misery of paupers meant that they were useless beings, "men good for nothing." On the contrary, he maintained, "beneath an exterior that may not be pleasing to the eye, there can be a soul of generous qualities. How do you or I know that among the poor seeking help there are not persons superior to us?"[21] And more importantly, the poor themselves, freed from the temptations posed by the possession of worldly goods, were the instruments designed by providence for the salvation of others. They were "the poor of Christ," the representatives of the Lord on earth whose prayers and supplications were efficacious precisely because of their poverty. The rich needed the poor to be saved, for according to Antonio Arbiol, "the prayers of the poor to whom you have given alms will rise to the ears of the God who will judge you."[22]

This theology of charity, it must be admitted, fitted well into a hierarchical social order divided into the three great estates of the old regime. The social contract between the privileged and the poor did not envisage the redistribution of wealth; it simply demanded that the rich should share some of their worldly goods with the impoverished. Even advocates of charity tempered their exhortations to the social and economic position of the individual. How much the rich were expected to give was not left entirely to personal initiative. According to Pedro de Calatayud, once an individual had met the cost of his basic necessities, he should spend a fourth or a third of what remained on the poor. The cost of those basic necessities, however, differed from one individual to another and depended, to use the critical phrase so often employed by the clerical moralists of the eighteenth century, on what remained after a person had spent enough to maintain "the decency of his state." This was a contract then operating within the confines of the established social order.

Moreover, not all Spaniards accepted the theory of charity outlined above, although few dared reject it outright. The increasing concern of government bureaucrats with economic problems during the eighteenth century led many to question the wisdom of a system in which charity was distributed on an indiscriminate basis to anyone asking for alms in the name of a purely spiritual goal. The state, supported by some churchmen, took up an idea that had first gained currency in the sixteenth century, the distinction between the "true" and "false" poor, and made it the basis of state policy during the reign of Charles III.[23] There could be no denial of the necessity of charity for religious purposes, but government administrators argued that many of those receiving alms were not truly poor but frauds and neer-do-wells who found that they did not have to work but could survive on the generosity of a Christian society. The creation of poorhouses, virtual prisons in fact, by the civil authorities, more vigorous police action against mendicants and the establishment of municipal charity boards during the second half of the century, all rested on the attempt to distinguish the "true" from the "false" poor. The former merited charity; the latter, punishment.

The state's poor relief policy foundered in part because of the resistance of upholders of the doctrine of "pure" charity, who tenaciously maintained that the social and economic effects of alms-giving were immaterial compared to the immense spiritual benefits which the act of giving alms brought to rich and poor alike. To distinguish among the poor on the basis of need in their view threatened the very structure of charity for religious motives. The archbishop of Burgos attacked those who refused to give charity on the grounds that many seeking help were "false" poor: "You are not an angel capable of discerning who is poor and who is not. You should not abandon the poor...simply because you suspect that some are only pretending to be impoverished."[24] An eighteenth-century bishop of Oviedo, when reproached for his gifts of alms because they contributed to laziness and the detriment of the public good, replied: "It is the part of the magistrate to clear the street of beggars; it is my duty to give alms to all who ask."[25] Opinion was especially hostile to the periodic police sweeps of beggars from city streets and their incarceration in poorhouses. Pedestrians frequently helped mendicants escape from the clutches of the police, and dislike of the poorhouses was general in the cities where they were established.[26] The archbishop of Burgos recalled that opinion in his diocesan seat regarded the local poorhouse "with pious horror...as a prison in which human liberty was imprisoned and charity made impossible," and in Alicante, the public regarded the *hospicios* as "houses of abomination."[27] Government measures to prevent the indiscriminate distribution of alms on the streets invariably failed during the late eighteenth century. In 1778, for example, the authorities of Madrid imposed severe restrictions on begging only to discover, to their despair, that mendicants continued to gather outside the city's churches to receive the gifts of a public more than willing to persist in its traditional generosity in spite of state regulations.[28]

The persistence of the traditional system of charity through the eighteenth century reveals the continuing vitality of the quasi-medieval social contract between the poor and the privileged. It may well have been significant in maintaining the social peace which historians have noted as one of the characteristics of eighteenth-century Spain, a period of few urban disturbances with the exception of a brief outburst in 1766. The maintenance of social tranquility, even in times of deep economic distress, was certainly not due to the traditional docility of the urban and rural populations, as the turbulence of Spanish history in the nineteenth century would show. It rested heavily, in my view, on the willingness of the Church and the privileged to uphold the terms of the social contract. By modern standards, of course, the religious poor relief of the eighteenth century fell short of being the kind of social welfare now judged acceptable. But within the limits set by the massive numbers of poor created by the weaknesses of the pre- industrial economy and the existence of a traditional society of orders, it functioned at least well enough to avoid starvation and total misery. It was, moreover, a system of public assistance depending on the personal rather than the institutional expression of the charitable impulse, the direct contact of the donor with the pauper; hence the common phenomenon in eighteenth-century Spain, so startling to foreign visitors, of bishops personally distributing alms to the poor gathered outside their gates, of grandees of Spain, representatives of the wealthiest and most distinguished noble houses of the kingdom, giving alms to the impoverished living in the squalid tenements of Madrid. The personal quality of religious charity was clearly one of its greatest strengths for it provided a highly visible manifestation of the support of the privileged for their side of the social contract. It can be argued, indeed, that the continuing vitality of charity by the privileged classes provided the traditional social order with one of its most important bulwarks.

The traditional system of charity, however, began to disintegrate towards the close of the eighteenth century. Earlier government intervention in the field of poor relief in a punitive direction and the increased criticism of religious charity for its indiscriminate character by segments of enlightened opinion in the 1770s and 1780s indicated a shift in attitudes on social welfare, although such views did not seriously affect the old charitable structure. But after 1790 the latter began to fray badly at the edges, largely because of financial considerations which reduced the funds available for alms. In this period of recurring economic crises (1788-1790, 1793-1794, 1797-1798, 1803-1805), characterized by grain shortages and steeply rising food prices, the demand for assistance increased dramatically, precisely at the moment when the Church and related charitable institutions found themselves caught in the grip of serious fiscal troubles.[29] Few charitable institutions were able to increase their incomes to keep pace with the intense inflationary spiral that beset Spain during the 1790s. The finances of two of Madrid's most important charitable bodies, the brotherhood of the Refugio, and the Inclusa or foundling hospital, were on the verge of collapse by 1800, and the Church itself, forced into massive contributions to the state to pay for Spain's defence in the midst of the international turmoil created by the Revolutionary and Napoleonic wars, witnessed the steady erosion of its resources. The ever more precarious condition of royal finances finally compelled the state to take the most drastic action yet taken against the traditional charitable order when, between 1805 and 1807, it ordered the sale of the property of hospitals, orphanages and charitable associations, the *hermandades*, *cofradías* and *congregaciones*, so important to the structure of urban poor relief.[30] The state's motives, although purely financial in this instance, dealt a blow to the old system of charity, which had come to depend heavily on donations of property, especially urban real estate, left by pious benefactors.

The breakdown of traditional mechanisms to deal with the poor was incomplete in 1808, the year Napolean replaced the Spanish Bourbons with a member of his own family, Joseph Bonaparte. That fateful decision plunged Spain into five years of war, constitutional revolution and internal chaos which destroyed the ability of the Church and the privileged to observe the terms of the social contract with the poor. In Toledo, the richest diocese of the Spanish church, the outbreak of war in 1808 so diminished revenues that ecclesiastical charity collapsed.[31] In Madrid, charitable brotherhoods saw income fall by more than two-thirds between 1808 and 1809.[32] Moreover, the hostility of the new French regime to the religious orders led to the closing of monasteries and convents throughout the kingdom, thereby eliminating another important source of assistance for the poor. The disintegration of the old charitable order could not have occurred at a worse time, for misery and, in some cases, famine were widespread between 1808 and 1813. During the ferocious winter of 1811-12 more than 20,000 persons were thought to have perished in Madrid alone, and there was little the civil authorities or the city's charitable institutions could do.[33]

With the restoration of absolute monarchy and the institutions of the old regime in 1814, the traditional system of charity recovered, but only partially. The destruction caused by long years of war left ecclesiastical revenues far below the level of 1800; by 1823, the income of the Toledo diocese was fifty percent lower than it had been before 1800. The Church attempted to resume its charitable activities, but its deteriorating finances prevented it from doing so completely. The same was true of the monasteries and convents re-established in 1814, for few were able to recover their former prosperity. The recovery, moreover, was interrupted by the liberal revolution of 1820, which endangered the traditional charitable structure once again. With the end of the liberal experiment in 1823, the charity of the Church and the privileged resumed, but in pale imitation of the past. By the death of Ferdinand VII in 1833, it had become obvious that the social contract between the privileged and the poor had broken down. In the summer of 1834, in the midst of an economic crisis of serious proportions, crowds in Madrid, Barcelona and other cities did not turn to the Church and charity to relieve their distress as they had

114

done so often in the past but rioted against them. Monasteries were set to the torch, and a number of religious murdered in the first great outbreak of anti-clerical violence in modern Spanish history.

The liberal attack on the property of the Church and charitable institutions beginning in 1835 destroyed once and for all a system of poor relief conducted for religious motives. Liberals saw social welfare in secular and philanthropic terms and installed a system of public assistance controlled by the state, in place of the charity of the Church and the associations engaged in relief for spiritual purposes. The end of the old social contract between the Church, the nobility and the poor, moreover, contributed to weakening the traditional hierarchical social order. The disappearance of charity deprived the Church of a social mechanism that for centuries had made the lower classes, especially those of the towns, dependent on it. Spanish history after 1834, with its recurring pattern of urban violence directed often against the ecclesiastical establishment, revealed how dangerously exposed the position of the Church had become.

William J. Callahan

Notes

1. For a succinct summary of disentailment, see F. Tomás y Valiente, *El marco politico de la desamortización en España* (Barcelona, 1971).

2. *Religiosidad de Cádiz* (Cadiz. 1840), p. 3.

3. Joseph Townsend, *A Journey through Spain in the Years 1786 and 1787*, 2nd ed., 3 vols. (London, 1792), 3:16-17, 183.

4. *Ibid.*, 3:57.

5. Joaquín Tello Giménez, *Hermandades y cofradías establecidas en Madrid* (Madrid, 1942), *passim*.

6. The brotherhood of San Fernando recruited only "persons of quality," another charitable association of the capital only those "with entailed estates or any other properties of honour inherited by right of blood." *Constituciones y instrucciones de la Hermandad del Real Hospicio de Pobres Mendigos de Ave María y San Fernando* (Madrid, 1675), p. 52; *Constituciones de la Real Congregación Nacional de Beneficencia de las tres nobles provincias de Cantabria*, 2nd ed. (Madrid, 1852), p. 28.

7. A. López Ferreiro, *Historia de la Santa A.M. Iglesia de Santiago de Compostela*, 11 vols. (Santiago, 1898-1908), 10: 127-37; A. Meijide Pardo, "El hambre en Galicia y la obra asistencial del estamento eclesiástico compostelano," *Compostellanum* 10, no. 2 (1965): 222-38.

8. See, for example, Francisco Antonio Lorenzana, archbishop of Toledo,

"Memorial que los pobres de la diócesi de Toledo presentan a toda clase de personas," in *Cartas, edictos y otras obras sueltas* (Toledo, 1786): Francisco Alejandro Bocanegra, archbishop of Santiago, *Sermones*, 2nd ed., 2 vols. (Madrid, 1773), 1: 170-90.

9. Antonio Arbiol, *La familia regulada con doctrina de la sagrada escritura*, 7th ed. (Zaragoza, 1729), pp. 309ff; Gregorio Baca de Haro, *Empresas morales para explicación de los mandamientos de la ley de Dios*, 2 vols. (Valladolid, 1703), 1:142-45. See also the sections in eighteenth-century catechisms: Pedro de Calatayud, *Cathecismo práctico y mui util para la instrucción y enseñanza facil de los fieles*, 8th ed. (Seville, 1761), pp. 158-59; Rafael Lasala y Locela, *Catecismo mayor de la doctrina christiana* (Cervera, 1791), p. 335.

10. Jean Sarrailh, *La España ilustrada de la segunda mitad del siglo XVIII* (Mexico, 1957), p. 58.

11. Bocanegra, *Sermones*, 1:185.

12. Calatayud, *Doctrinas*, 2: 122.

13. Calatayud, *Cathecismo prácto*, p. 159.

14. Calatayud, *Doctrinas* 2:130.

15. *Ibid.*, 2:120.

16. Bocanegra, *Sermones*, 1:259-60.

17. Lorenzana, "Memorial que los pobres," no page numbers.

18. Calatayud, *Doctrinas*, 1:125.

19. Bocanegra, *Sermones*, 1:190.

20. Thus, Felipe Bertrán, the bishop of Salamanca, stressed the charitable obligation on the grounds that the poor formed part of the mystical body of Christ and had the same spiritual goal as others in society whatever their class. *Colección de las cartas pastorales y edictos*, 2 vols. (Madrid, 1783), 1:322.

21. Rodríguez Arellano, *Pastorales*, 5:491.

22. Arbiol, *La familia regulada*, p. 311.

23. For a brief discussion of the origins of this discussion, see María Jiménez Salas, *Historia de la asistencia social en España en la edad moderna* (Madrid, 1958), pp. 89-98.

24. Rodríguez Arellano, *Pastorales*, 5:491.

25. Townsend, *A Journey through Spain*, 2:9.

26. Tomás Anzano, *Elementos preliminares para poder formar un sistema de gobierno de hospicio general* (Madrid, 1778), p. 62.

27. Townsend, *A Journey through Spain*, 3: 183.

28. W.J. Callahan, "The Problem of Confinement: An Aspect of Poor Relief in Eighteenth-Century Spain," *Hispanic American Historical Review* 51, no. 1 (1971): 21.

29. Gonzalo Anés has ably described the ever more serious economic crises of the late eighteenth and early nineteenth centuries in *Las crisis agrarias en la España moderna* (Madrid, 1970), pp. 401ff.

30. Richard Herr has described the disentailing process before 1808 in "Hacia el derrumbe del Antiguo Régimen: crisis fiscal y desamortización fiscal bajo Carlos IV," *Moneda y crédito*, no. 118 (1971), pp. 37-100.

116

31. Leandro Higueruela del Pino, *El clero de la dióesis de Toledo durante el pontificado del cardenal Borbón* (Madrid, 1973), p. 10.

32. Income of the brotherhood of the Refugio, one of the capital's largest and wealthiest charitable groups, fell from 516,823 *reales* in 1808 to 167,306 *reales* in 1811. See Archivo de la Santa y Real Hermandad del Refugio y Piedad, Cuentas Generales, legs. 200-201.

33. Manuel Espada-Burgos, "El hambre de 1812 en Madrid," *Hispania* 28, no. 110 (1968): 610.

Ambiguity and Ambivalence:
The Plight of Eighteenth-Century Jewry
in Western Europe

The eighteenth century is of particular interest for Jewish historians since it witnessed the first major attempts to grapple with what we may call Jewish modernity: a Jewish existence isolated neither physically, politically, culturally nor socially from the non-Jewish environment. During the Enlightenment the central problem of modern diaspora Jewry — the preservation of Jewish identity in an inclusive milieu — arose significantly for the first time. The emergence of this new situation created a crisis, for it spawned uncertainty, anxiety and inner conflict, even as it raised new hope. The purpose of this article is to delineate and analyze some of the elements in this crisis.

I

It must first be noted that European Jewish history in the eighteenth century is the history of highly diverse Jewish communities. Not only did political circumstances differ markedly, but religious beliefs and practices did as well. In Eastern Europe, which contained by far the greatest number of Jews, the eighteenth century witnessed no noteworthy change from the medieval pattern of restriction and isolation. Jewish autonomy in internal affairs was accompanied by the perpetuation of traditional religious attitudes. After the mid-century, East European Jewry did suffer a major rift, brought about by the rise of Hasidism, a pietistic movement with enormous appeal, especially to the impoverished masses in the south. But if Hasidism provided a crisis of Judaism, it was almost wholly an internal one, unrelated to outside influences. Moreover, by the following century the controversy between the Hasidim and their opponents had paled as both sides joined in combatting a mounting secularism which their brethren in the West had faced much earlier.

It was only in the states of Central and Western Europe that Judaism underwent a genuine crisis in the eighteenth century, and even this assertion must be qualified. The crisis cannot be precisely located with regard to time — it varied, depending on the specific circumstances of Jewish communities in the West; it also did not affect all economic and social classes of Jewry to the same degree. Some of its aspects had already manifested themselves before the beginning of the century, and a uniform and lasting resolution of issues had most definitely not been reached at its conclusion. Yet in the course of the eighteenth century growing numbers of Jews in England, France and the Central European states were profoundly transformed — and troubled — by their exposure to the age of Enlightenment.

The crisis arose from developments outside the Jewish community. In the Middle Ages, Jews had been carefully set apart from a Christian society whose religious ideology called for a minimization of contact with them. During the eighteenth century that exclusionary ideology waned. The enclosed corporative Jewish entity came under attack both because it contradicted the policy of political centralization and because Enlightenment universalism demanded a fresh view of the Jews — not as Christ-killers, but as human beings. Jewish communities thus found themselves in an environment increasingly favourable to their integration. Yet even as their humanity was recognized, in literature, on the stage and in social circles, full acceptance of the Jews was regularly hedged by conditions. Gentiles questioned whether the Jews, unchanged, and Judaism, unreformed, deserved a place in modern society. There was widespread disagreement on what specific changes should be required, and there were many who held that integration was impossible without some form of conversion. The Jews themselves were perplexed by this diversity and ambiguity of attitude. They were unsure what was expected of them and ambivalent in their own attitudes and feelings. Among themselves, they, too, differed widely on the extent to which they believed Jews and Judaism would have to change. Those who increasingly identified with the intellectual and social world outside Judaism began to loosen their connections with fellow Jews, especially with those who differed most from themselves. They took a fresh look at their tradition, now under attack, not as in the past by sworn enemies, but as apparent friends. Some denied or minimized certain of the inherited tenets of Judaism, and many found themselves no longer emotionally attached to its full range of religious expression. The quandary was how to live as a Jew within a society which recognized the Jew's potential humanity but criticized his present moral state, which either venerated or despised the Hebrew Bible but in either case had little regard for contemporary Judaism, which enticed and sometimes rebuffed him but was influencing him ever more — driving him either to defend, to restructure or to abandon his faith.

II

The Jewish community in England illustrates most aspects of this situation. Of all the major European Jewish settlements before the French Revolution, the Jews of England enjoyed the highest degree of political and economic freedom. They were also the newest community. For three-and-a half centuries following their expulsion by Edward I in 1290, there had been no officially recognized Jewish community in England. Only at the time of Oliver Cromwell did a tiny, surreptitious congregation of refugees from Spain and Portugal dare to reveal its true religion. Beginning in 1656, Jewish public worship in England once again became legal, and thereafter Jews from the continent crossed the Channel in increasing numbers seeking to share in the benefits of England's rapid economic progress. As the historian Cecil Roth has emphasized, the fact that Jewish existence in England was simply legitimized, without the conclusion of a charter delineating rights and restrictions, created a Jewish community which from the outset was not set apart by specific exclusionary legislation.[1] In this respect it differed notably from the pattern on the Continent. The political discrimination which Jews suffered in England involved only exclusion from such privileges as were reserved to members of the established Church. They could live wherever they wanted, they were not required to pay special taxes imposed only on Jews, and they were rarely subjected to the violence of a mob.

However, the legally undefined character of Jewish status in England was not an unmixed blessing. If ever an anti-Jewish movement should arise, it would not be difficult to question whether Jews did in fact have the right of residence. Unlike their far more restricted brethren in Italy, for example, they would then be unable to prove their rights through any English equivalent of a Venetian *condotta* guaranteeing contracted privileges until the date of its expiration.

The Jews of England were well aware of just how unsure their status was. From the beginning it was the resolute policy of the community to maintain a "low profile." Its regulations strictly prohibited members from discussing religious subjects with Gentiles or speaking derogatorily of their faith, "because to do otherwise is to disturb the liberty which we enjoy and to make us disliked." The greatest potential danger was seen to lie in the anticipated angry reaction to Jewish proselytism. Such activity was likewise strictly forbidden by the community's laws, and the prohibition was reemphasized in a resolution of 1751 that threatened violators with expulsion from the synagogue and denial of Jewish burial.[2] A considerable portion of the community's budget was devoted to *douceurs* that were delivered regularly, or as the need arose, to prominent public officials. Pursuing a policy of deliberately avoiding attention while quietly working to dismantle economic barriers, the early Jewish community hoped that the mere passage of time and the gradual integration of Jews into the social fabric of England would secure their loosely determined position.

A very specific and apparently unforeseen crisis in the middle of the eighteenth century almost upset this strategy. On Jewish initiative a naturalization act, known popularly as the "Jew Bill," was introduced into Parliament in 1753. Its provisions were hardly such as were expected to arouse great opposition. They were designed simply to make it possible for foreign Jews residing in England to gain naturalization by exempting them from the requirement of taking the sacrament. Immigrant Jews would thus be enabled to apply to Parliament for a private act to free them from the economic disabilities that applied generally to foreigners and which were not shared by Jews born in England. The Jew Bill passed the House of Lords without dissent but encountered considerable opposition in the Commons. Although it eventually passed there by a comfortable margin, the question of somewhat expanded Jewish rights which it raised proved an extremely volatile issue. When the Tory opposition exploited it to arouse the public against the Whig government in a forthcoming general election, the Pelham ministry had no choice but to seek the law's immediate repeal.

The clamour raised by debate over the Jew Bill proved that the Jewish community's fears had been well justified. A "sleeping dog" had been stirred to life. For months the controversy raged in the newspapers, the magazines and in some sixty or so published pamphlets — the vast majority of them hostile to the Jews. Medieval charges enjoyed a new vogue: not only had the Jews once crucified the son of God, but if contemporary Jews had him in their power they would crucify him once more; Jews were sworn enemies of Christianity, properly to be viewed in accordance with the Gospel of John as children of the devil.[3] Such charges were not limited to the foreign-born Jews affected by the bill; they were hurled without distinction at those families long settled in England as well. One opponent in Parliament indeed wondered whether a secret committee should not be appointed "to enquire, whether the Jews be allowed to have a synagogue, or other place of public worship in this Kingdom and if they have by what authority that indulgence has been granted or allowed."[4] It seemed as if only a spark had been required to fire the tinder of mistrust and ill-will which had been smoldering all the while.

True to their principles, the Jewish leaders remained in the background. They did not openly defend the bill themselves, preferring to express their sentiments through a Gentile writer and agent, and perhaps through one or two of the anonymous pamphlets. Fortunately, the clamour died down speedily after repeal, and English Jewry emerged with no diminution of its status. But it was severely shaken and was henceforth hesitant about initiating further efforts to broaden Jewish equality, regardless of how innocuous they might seem. As a result, the last obstacle to Jewish political equality in Britain (the Christian oath required of members of Parliament) was removed only in 1858, long after similar barriers had fallen elsewhere in Europe.

III

The debate over the Jew Bill was not only a political crisis for Anglo-Jewry; it also brought into focus an underlying social and religious crisis which had begun considerably before the frenzy of 1753 and did not end when it subsided. The action of one prominent individual is illustrative. Samson Gideon was one of England's leading financiers and the trusted counsellor of successive governments. A native-born Jew of Spanish-Portuguese stock, his greatest desire, once he had achieved an enormous fortune, was to gain a peerage and thus add aristocracy to affluence. He married a Christian woman and insisted that each of his children be baptized by the sub-dean of St. Paul's, though he himself remained nominally Jewish. Unlike his fellow Jews, Gideon did not support the Jew Bill. The reason for his opposition is not known, though one may surmise that his identification with his co-religionists, especially those from abroad, had so far diminished that he was little concerned to advance their welfare. Nonetheless, the Jewish community apparently used his name in connection with their efforts on behalf of the bill. In the midst of the debate, Gideon's familiar figure appeared in caricature offering a bag of money to the government. Exceedingly indignant, he decided to make an official break with the Spanish and Portuguese Synagogue, declaring in his letter of resignation: "You know the matter solicited for, to be directly contrary to my declared Sentiments, and my dislike to all Innovations."[5] Although Gideon continued anonymously to pay his congregational dues and left funds for his burial in the Jewish cemetery, this most prominent English Jew of his day had become so estranged from his fellow Jews that at a time of public clamour against them he would not share their burden. The cause of the Jews was no longer his own.

The case of Samson Gideon was far from isolated. During the eighteenth century, the wealthier Jews of the second and third generations became increasingly anglicized, rendering tenuous or cutting entirely their ties with the Jewish community. A situation emerged in which the most prominent and wealthy families became the furthest removed from the synagogue — when indeed they did not go so far as to intermarry or themselves convert to Christianity. Within the Sephardi (the Spanish and Portuguese) community, the leading names of the seventeenth century were no longer on the rolls by the end of the eighteenth. In part, this process of assimilation and concurrent alienation was due to the relatively hospitable social environment. Wealthy Jews, in particular, might expect to be treated with respect and dignity in non-Jewish circles; once they had learned the English language, developed artistic and literary taste and adopted English customs and habits, they found few barriers to social integration. But in part, assimilation and alienation were due also to the continuing insecurity of being a Jew.

This process of estrangement was hastened and radicalized in England by the inflexibility of the Spanish and Portuguese synagogue. The strict regulations which it imposed on its members had been the product of fears quite understandable among refugees from the Inquisition. However, the Sephardi leadership assumed that unyielding authoritarian control over each individual, which had appeared necessary to safeguard the fledgling community, would also serve as a bulwark against a rising tide of social and intellectual integration. Throughout the eighteenth century the community leadership tried to combat assimilation with insulation. It repeatedly refused to allow private gatherings for prayer, fining and humiliating those who dared to violate its statutes. Spanish and Portuguese continued to be the languages of sermons and synagogue records; the board of the congregation consistently refused to allow publication of the prayers in English translation. Although attendance decreased markedly, the service itself remained wholly unchanged. By the second half of the century, community offices (which involved possible financial liability) were frequently refused by those to whom they were offered. For many of the members, the synagogue had become religiously irrelevant, and they were now seeking and receiving social gratification elsewhere.

The gap between the Jewish and non-Jewish worlds might have been narrowed had there been a rabbinic leadership capable of constructing an intellectual bridge. However, the English Jewish community in the eighteenth century produced no Jewish thinker desirous or capable of harmonizing Judaism with current philosophy. The most prominent religious writer in Anglo-Jewry of the period was Haham David Nieto, who served as rabbi of the Sephardi Jewish congregation in London from 1701 to 1728.[6] He had come to England from Italy after studying medicine at Padua and serving the Jewish community in Leghorn as preacher, judge and physician. Nieto was quite familiar with classical writers, with the natural sciences and apparently also with contemporary philosophy. Yet he used his wide knowledge to uphold a position that made no concessions to the currents of his time. On the contrary, his writings and sermons were often a sharp polemic against the critics of any aspect of Jewish tradition. For Nieto the written law of the Bible and the oral law of the rabbis were wholly the word of God. Even the rabbinic *aggada*, with all its extravagant interpretations and incredible anecdotes, was true in every detail. Had not travellers in his own day told similar astounding stories? Nieto was apparently aware of deistic notions, either directly or through hearing them in conversation. He may even have derived one of his arguments for the existence of God, that *de consensu gentium*, from the deists. But he absolutely rejected their conception of a creator God removed from an autonomously functioning nature. In one sermon, which prompted a major controversy in the congregation, Nieto defended an identification of nature with God's providence, quite unintentionally leading some of his listeners mistakenly to believe that he leaned toward Spinozism.

Nieto never became part of the English intellectual world. Despite his wide knowledge of languages, he did not quickly master English. Such contacts as he had with educated Christians seem to have been limited to traditionally inclined scholars.[7] Certainly there was a fraction of the congregation which Nieto served very well. They wanted a man versed in secular knowledge — which was considered an honourable achievement among the Sephardim — but one who would champion traditional belief and practice. There were others, however, who could not accept such a stance for themselves. Dr. Jacob de Castro Sarmiento, a close friend of Nieto who had once substituted for him in the pulpit and who later became a Fellow of the Royal Society, resigned from the congregation some years after Nieto's death because, as he wrote, "The different opinions and sentiments I have entertained long ago, entirely dissenting from those of the Synagogue, do not permit me any longer to keep the appearance of a member of your body..."[8] With increasing defection for social and for intellectual reasons, the Sephardi leadership responded simply by reaffirming the old ways more forcefully and more dogmatically — to an ever-diminishing number of listeners.

IV

By the end of the eighteenth century the Spanish and Portuguese Jews in London constituted only about one-fifth of the city's Jewish population. The great bulk were now Ashkenazim: Jews from Holland, Germany and Poland who had sought economic opportunity and a more secure existence in England. With a few notable exceptions, the Ashkenazi community was considerably poorer than the Sephardi: its ranks swelled from year to year by penniless immigrants who threw themselves on the mercies of fellow Jews, most of whom were only slightly better off than they were. Barred from retail trade in London, they engaged in such occupations as peddling in town and countryside or mending and reselling old clothes. These impoverished immigrants, arriving later than the Iberian Jews and initially speaking Yiddish, seem to have been relatively less subject to the assimilatory enticements that affected the wealthy Sephardi families. Their undistinguished religious leadership during this period could thus remain as unyielding in its own way as that of the Sephardim without the same immediate consequences.

Relations between Sephardim and Ashkenazim had never been very good. From the time that Iberian Jews began their flight eastwards, following their expulsion from Spain in 1492, they had stringently kept themselves apart from the Ashkenazim they encountered. It was the pattern for each community to have its own synagogues and religious functionaries. In some places each had a separate charter of privileges and restrictions from the government. Throughout Europe the Sephardim were the wealthier, and they generally enjoyed a broader education. With considerable hauteur they looked down upon their poorer and — they thought — culturally inferior brethren from Central and Eastern Europe.

In eighteenth-century England demographic change served to exacerbate this separatism. As the Sephardi community was transformed from a preponderant majority to a small minority, the public image of the Jew came to be shaped increasingly by the more visible German or Polish peddler. Caricatures at the time of the Jew Bill protrayed all Jews — even the Sephardim — as speaking English with a Yiddish accent. The Anglo-Jewish *hidalgos* recoiled from such depictions and stressed ever more vigorously their separate and distinct identity. They also felt less obligation to provide for the needs of the Ashkenazi poor. When a comprehensive project for relief of the indigent was proposed in 1802, it came to nought on account of the wealthier Sephardi community's refusal to assume a share of the burden proportionate to its financial capacities.

A similar distinction gradually arose in England between native and foreign-born Jews. As anglicization progressed, the sense of obligation towards Jews outside the country weakened. Especially those who might prove a financial liability were discouraged from immigration. Undesirables included both the poorer Sephardim from North Africa and the Levant as well as — and especially — penniless Ashkenazim from Eastern Europe. In 1771 the Ashkenazi community went so far as to express its gratitude to the Home Office for attempting to exclude those Jewish immigrants from Poland who could not afford the usual passenger freight on the packet boats.[9] Given a relatively favourable environment, a distinctly English Jewish identity was developing which came greatly to weaken — though not to displace entirely — the sense of common Jewish destiny which had prevailed earlier.

V

The drift towards a more narrowly perceived Jewish identity was apparent also on the Continent. Here the desire to limit one's Jewish reference group was brought about less by demographic change than by literary slurs and an uncertain momentum toward political emancipation. Like English Jewry, the Jews of France in the eighteenth century were also divided into Sephardi and Ashkenazi communities, differentiated economically and culturally. But in the case of France there was an additional distinction: the two groups were geographically separated. The Ashkenazim lived in the region of Alsace in the east of France, while the much smaller Sephardi population was settled in Bordeaux and Bayonne.

In his *Philosophical Dictionary* Voltaire had written of the Jews in general that they were an "ignorant and barbarous people who have long united the most sordid avarice with the most detestable superstition and the most invincible hatred for every people by whom they are tolerated and enriched."[10] In response, Isaac de Pinto, a Sephardi Jew of France and Holland, contended that Voltaire's strictures might well apply to the Ashkenazim (since the contempt in which they were held had had the effect of crushing their every germ of virtue and honour), but it was certainly in error with regard to the Sephardim. Pinto noted:

> A Jew of London resembles a Jew of Constantinople as little as the latter resembles a Chinese mandarin. A Portuguese Jew of Bordeaux and a German Jew of Metz are absolutely different from each other. It is therefore not possible to speak of Jewish manners and customs in general, without entering into great detail and specific distinctions. The Jew is a chameleon, who takes on all the colours of the different regions which he inhabits, the different peoples with whom he comes into contact, and the different forms of government under which he lives.[11]

Pinto noted that Voltaire should have begun by distinguishing the Spanish and Portuguese Jews from the "common herd of Jacob's other descendants." Sephardi Jews, he observed, wore no beards, dressed according to fashion, and differed from other Europeans only with regard to religious worship. Pinto was eager that Voltaire and his other Christian readers know that a Portuguese Jew marrying a German Jewess in Holland or England was thereby excluded from the synagogue and not even interred among his brethren. Sephardi Jews, to be sure, had their faults as well, but they differed from those of the Ashkenazim: ostentation, vanity, a passion for women, a contempt for physical labour, a supercilious pride. These, he wrote, were the "vices of noble spirits."

Such separatist sentiments were shared by Pinto's associates. Twenty-seven years later, in 1789, the Sephardi lay leaders in France tried to prevent an immediate grant of full citizenship to the Ashkenazim. And, in fact, the Spanish and Portuguese in France were emancipated in January 1790, while their fellow Alsatian Jews had to wait another year and a half until September 1791. Only when Napoleon established a single consistory for both groups in 1808 did the French Jewish community begin to see itself as one.

VI

The Sephardi withdrawal was but one response to continuing hostility: its deflection to Jews beyond the principal group of identification. Among Jews on the Continent, the ambiguous environment of the eighteenth century brought forth more complex responses to what became a crisis both of faith and of self-esteem. After the Thirty-Years War, a thin upper stratum of Jewry, the "Court Jews," had gained access not only to considerable wealth, but also to the social milieu of the nobility. From the wealthiest, this increased exposure broadened to other strata of the Jewish community including especially those whose intellectual curiosity brought them into contact with the writings of the Enlightenment. As their ties to the outside world grew stronger, an increasing number of Jews were exposed to its values and gradually came to internalize them. When these conflicted with accustomed belief and practice, a dilemma was created which split the Jewish community not into two, but into a spectrum of views, ranging from those who favoured abandoning Judiasm entirely, through reformers of varying degrees, to champions of tradition who would venture few concessions, if any.

As long as orthodox Christianity prevailed, whether in Catholic or Protestant form, the Jews were regarded as a despised people rejected by God, properly to be isolated from Christian society. What Jews specifically believed and practised mattered little provided they did not malign Christianity. But once this doctrine of Jewish separation was challenged on political and moral grounds, Jews were faced with a new and uncertain reality. Some were soon willing, even eager, to give up entirely their separate ways of life in order to become fully Germans or Frenchmen. Others questioned whether it was advisable to yield the emotional and intellectual security of ghetto existence, doubting whether Judaism could flourish as an exposed minority faith in an environment of complete political, economic, social and intellectual integration. Those in the middle wanted Judaism to survive as a separate entity in some form but differed in their vision of its modernized character.

The Jewish writers who dealt with these issues had to take full account of the views that had been expressed by non-Jews. Both traditional and Enlightenment thinkers had cast doubts on the compatibility of Judaism with modern intellectual principles, with enlightened moral values and with civic responsibilities. Almost all of them had held that Jews and Judaism in their present form were not acceptable. Jews as human beings possessed faults of character; their faith was at best superstitious, at worst barbaric.

Anti-Jewish arguments coming from reactionary opponents of Jewish integration did not create the crisis. The problem came from those writers who championed toleration and intellectual advance — with whose general principles many Jews themselves therefore identified — but who derided or condemned Jewish characteristics, beliefs and practices. The English deists, whose writings were widely read in both France and Germany, nearly all attacked Judaism.[12] They were advocates of toleration but, with few exceptions, such as John Toland and William Wollaston,[13] they deprecated biblical and rabbinic tradition. Their opposition to all positive religion, and especially to exclusive claims, led them to revile doctrines at the heart of Judaism: the election of Israel, the observance of divinely ordained ritual commandments and the messianic hope. Some saw the Jewish heritage as responsible for all the defects of Christianity. Leading writers of the Enlightenment in France were generally even more critical. Beginning with

Pierre Bayle they scoffed at rabbinic tradition, fastening upon the most extravagant hyperboles and holding them up to ridicule.[14] Voltaire relished pointing out the barbarities perpetrated by Old Testament Jews; their descendants were foolish — or worse — to cling to so immoral and ludicrous a faith. If they suffered on its account, that was partly at least their own fault. As the Sage of Ferney put it, with typical irony: "By an incomprehensible providence of the Supreme Being you have been the most unfortunate of all men since you became the most faithful..."[15]

Because of their commitment to universal toleration, most Enlightenment thinkers favoured eventual acceptance of the Jews. But the Jews would have to be transformed. The *philosophers*, too, expected the Jews to convert, not to Christianity, but to the God of reason. Once again Voltaire, in reply to Isaac de Pinto, "As you are a Jew, remain so. You will never cut the throats of 42,000 men because they pronounced the word Shibboleth wrong, nor destroy 24,000 men for having lain with the Midianite women. But be a philosopher. This is my best wish to you in this short life."[16] Even the best friends of the Jews demanded or simply presumed that Judaism would not remain as it was. Christian Wilhelm Dohm, perhaps the foremost German proponent of Jewish equality, wrote in 1781 that the "anxious and petty spirit of ceremonialism, which has insinuated itself into the present-day Jewish religion, will surely disappear again as soon as wider horizons are opened to the Jews, once they are accepted as members of the polity and can make its interest their own. Then they, in turn, will appropriately recast their religious constitution and laws..."[17] In his *Lettres juives*, the Marquis d'Argens depicted three *philosophes Hébreux* who had overcome all superstitions including the Jewish one, while Lessing in his *Nathan der Weise* created a model Jew, scarcely believable to many Christians, but as much a paradigm for Jewish enlighteners as was Moses Mendelssohn, the real-life figure who suggested the character. The Abbé Grégoire, a principal advocate of Jewish emancipation in France, looked forward to a process of assimilation so complete that it would ultimately result in all Jews becoming Catholics.

Influenced by a variety of motives — the quests for economic advance, for social acceptance and prestige and for the diminution of antisemitic hostility, as well as a genuinely felt desire to be modern men — a growing number of Jews began to divest themselves of those beliefs and practices which seemed to offend non-Jews. But it was not merely a matter of paying a stated price for emancipation. Not only was there no agreement as to demands, but such a notion implies that, given a choice, the Jews would have preferred to receive political and social equality while remaining as they were. In fact, the situation was so difficult for those Jews most exposed to outside opinions of Judaism precisely because, to varying degrees, they were coming to share those same views. Some of them were as alienated from traditional Judaism as the men of the Enlightenment were from orthodox Christianity. The *philosophes* and the *Aufklärer* were setting an example by their treatment of the Christian tradition. Even had they written nothing specifically to denigrate Judaism, the Jewish enlighteners, the *maskilim*, would not have refrained from directing a similar critique at their own faith.

The process of estrangement from traditional Judaism, which repeated itself in each generation, began with small numbers in the West towards the middle of the eighteenth century, then broadened and eventually reached Eastern Europe. It consisted basically of three steps: first, exposure to the intellectual values and the social mores of non-Jewish society; second, identification with the values found outside of Judaism and often in conflict with it; and third, judgment of Jewish institutions, traditions and beliefs in the light of those values.

The new orientation which thus emerged could be seen, for example, in an altered conception of religious leadership. The rabbinate in the eighteenth century had maintained its medieval character. Its leading figures continued to be concerned with upholding Judaism in unchanged form, violently opposing innovation in belief and practice. As the designated guardians of tradition, they utilized whatever authority and influence was available to them in order to maintain religious conformity. But in Central and Western Europe the influence of the rabbinate was ebbing rapidly. A protracted and bitter dispute between two leading rabbis (Jacob Emden and Jonathan Eibeschütz) — both opponents of modernization, but the one a rationalist and the other an apparent adherent to the Sabbatian heresy — enlarged disrespect for the institution and resentment at its continuing claims to authority. Even Moses Mendelssohn, a fully observant Jew, argued along with the enlightened non-Jewish thinkers of his age for allowing religion to be a private matter and against the assertion of ecclesiastical authority in any religious community. Rabbis were to persuade, not to wield the sword of excommunication. More extreme writers, such as Zalkind-Hourwitz, concluded that the rabbinate was an unnecessary and irrelevant luxury, a damaging institution because it was an unnecessary and irrelevant luxury, a damaging institution because it was devoted to opposing all change. "It would even be desirable," he wrote on the eve of the Revolution, "if one would prohibit [the Jews] from employing rabbis, whose support is so expensive and who are absolutely useless. For they never officiate in the synagogue and only preach twice a year. Moreover, their sermons merely revolve around obscure passages in the Talmud or they cast about for subtleties of which nine-tenths of their listeners understand not one word."[18] It was not until the first decades of the nineteenth century that there emerged a university-educated religious leadership, fulfilling a role largely analogous to that of the Christian clergy. To the degree that these new men, whether orthodox or liberal, were able to address themselves to the altered situation, they succeeded in restoring the rabbinate (though never completely) to a position of some respect and influence.

During the eighteenth century, new conceptions of Judaism came not from the constituted religious authorities but from laymen, some of them well versed in Jewish tradition, others not, but all deeply influenced by the intellectual and social environment outside of Judaism. Moses Mendelssohn's solution to the problem of redefining Judaism is well known. He held that it consisted first, of eternal verities determinable by reason and not limited to any specific revelation; second, of historical truths, events attested to by eye witnesses; and third, of divine legislation given to the Jews at Sinai but binding upon them alone and not requisite for the salvation of non-Jews. With the exception of certain, "worthless volumes," Mendelssohn publicly upheld the totality of Jewish tradition, simply reinterpreting it selectively to stress its rational and universalistic elements. In its basic tenets it became natural religion, while its particularity was removed from the area of theological doctrines and limited to observance of the ceremonial law.[19]

More radical thinkers became convinced that far more was required. In an essay published in 1793, when he was living in Vienna, the German Jewish mathematician, philosopher and educator, Lazarus Bendavid, declared that Prussian and Austrian

Jewry now fell into four categories: those who remained loyal to the enormous mass of Jewish traditions (still by far the largest class); those who for strictly opportunistic reasons had ceased to be observant; those who no longer believed in traditional Judaism but feared the moral consequences of abandoning it; and, finally, the followers of the "pure Mosaic doctrine," which Bendavid equated with genuine natural religion. The last group had abandoned the "shameful, senseless ceremonial law," and it no longer regarded talmudic tradition as authoritative.[20] What Bendavid failed to indicate in regard to this last group — his own — was the nature of its Jewish particularity. He had put forward a statement of faith with no links whatever to Jewish tradition except for the questionable supposition that Moses was the father of rational faith.

In France, too, there was a felt need to answer political and intellectual criticisms and to put forward acceptable conceptions of Judaism. In the midst of public debate over Jewish emancipation just before and during the French Revolution, Jewish writers and petitioners were pressed to explain how Judaism, as they understood it or as they desired to see it transformed, was compatible with French citizenship. They responded by pointing out that, while Jews awaited the Messiah (as they awaited death!), their millenial hope did not prevent them from building houses and accepting responsibilities, and that it would not diminish their political loyalty. Like Mendelssohn, they especially stressed Judaism's universalism and tolerance. All men were worthy of salvation if they but observed the fundamental religious and moral principles represented by the Seven Commandments which, according to Jewish tradition, God had given to Noah.[21] If Jews possessed the vices ascribed to them by opponents of their emancipation, such faults did not derive from their faith but from the history of restriction and persecution which they had undergone. Judaism itself was not a corrupter of innate human viture but served to enhance it. Since mid-century, Mendelssohn, had presented the parade example of a virtuous Jew, who combined faithfulness to Judaism with universally recognized integrity and philosophical wisdom. In the last decade of the century, French apologists for Judaism sought to show that, were Judaism allowed to flourish within modern society, it would produce more Jews like him, inculcating the young with precisely those virtues requisite for citizenship. Yet there was some ambivalence on this point since not all writers were equally convinced that Judaism could in fact be so easily transported from the ghetto into the midst of a single *communauté touchante*. Zalkind-Hourwitz, for example, felt constrained to emphasize its innocuousness: "La Religion n'influe point sur presque tous les actes des Juifs."[22] He also noted that Jews disregarded rabbinic tradition on just those points most vulnerable to criticism on moral grounds.

The specific criticisms of Enlightenment writers were answered in three ways. First, Jewish authors corrected in detail intentional or innocent misinterpretations of the Bible and Talmud. Second, they compared barbarities or inanities in Jewish tradition with parallels in classical antiquity and Christianity; third, they declared non-normative or reinterpreted those prescriptions and prohibitions with which they could not themselves agree. That still left the task of defining for non-Jews and for themselves just what the essence of Judaism was. One definition, representative of the period, is contained in a petition to the National Assembly of the year 1790. It cast Jewish faith into a mould unexceptionable but to the most radical of *philosophes*. Judaism possessed only three basic dogmas: the unity of God, the immortality of the soul and future reward and punishment (not the chosenness of Israel, not the hope of messianic restoration to the Land). Likewise, Jewish practice consisted of only three principal rites: circumcision, the Sabbath and the Jewish festivals.[23] Such a rational and limited religion, it must have been thought, would meet little objection from the outside world and could serve as a common denominator within.

VII

Stripped to essentials, drawing only selectively on its tradition, transforming itself from a community governed by religious law into a community of individual faith and cultic practice, Judaism in the West emerged from the eighteenth century very different from what it had been at its beginning. An atmosphere ambiguously hostile and friendly had siphoned off into Christianity those Jews whose economic and social progress had most loosened their connections with fellow Jews and who were unwilling to forego the established status and security which they believed would come through absorption into the majority. It had exacerbated the dissociation between Sephardim and Ashkenazim and brought to the fore a distinction between native and foreign Jews. In an intellectual environment increasingly tolerant of the Jew as a human being but suspicious of his Judaism, and at a time when the values of the Enlightenment were penetrating ever more deeply into the Jewish community itself, defenders of Judaism, who were themselves in varying degrees ambivalent towards the tradition, were at pains to refocus Judaism upon these points which were most generally acceptable both to their own religious sensibilities and to non-Jewish opinion. This task could not be done in any one manner which would be acceptable to more than a segment of the Jewish community, even in a particular country. Some solutions — like that of Mendelssohn — would not outlive a single generation; others would survive as elements in new constellations. By the end of the eighteenth century, Judaism in the West possessed a direction of response to its new situation, but it did not speak in a single voice. In the following decades, religious and ideological division among Jews would be accentuated even further. The plight of eighteenth-century Jewry in the West — the crisis produced by increasing but often anxious contact with a changing and itself contradictory milieu — was to characterize Jewish history down to the present time.

Michael A. Meyer

Notes

1. Cecil Roth, *Essays and Portraits in Anglo-Jewish History* (Philadelphia, 1962), pp. 86-107; *idem, A History of the Jews in England*, 3rd ed. (Oxford, 1964), pp. 149-72.

2. James Picciotto, *Sketches of Anglo-Jewish History* (London, 1875), pp. 36-38, 78-79; Albert H. Hyamson, *The Sephardim of England* (London, 1951), pp. 29, 174-75.

3. See, for example, *A Modest Apology for the Citizens and Merchants of London Who Petitioned the House of Commons against Naturalizing the Jews* (London, 1753). The pamphlets are listed in Cecil Roth, *Magna Bibliotheca Anglo-Judaica* (London, 1937), pp. 215-25.

4. Quoted in Thomas W. Perry, *Public Opinion, Propaganda, and Politics in Eighteenth-Century England: A Study of the Jew Bill of 1753* (Cambridge, Mass., 1962), p. 87.

5. Quoted in Cecil Roth, ed., *Anglo-Jewish Letters* (London, 1938), pp. 130-32. See also L.S. Sutherland, "Samson Gideon: Eighteenth Century Jewish Financier," *Jewish Historical Society of England Transactions* 17 (1953): 79-90.

6. On Nieto, see especially Jakob J. Petuchowski, *The Theology of Haham David Nieto*, rev. ed. (New York, 1970).

7. Roth, *Essays and Portraits*, pp. 119-20.

8. Quoted in Petuchowski, *Nieto*, p. 22.

9. G.B. Hertz, *British Imperialism in the Eighteenth Century* (London, 1908), p. 102.

10. See Shmuel Ettinger, "Jews and Judaism as Seen by the English Deists of the 18th Century" (in Hebrew), *Zion* 39 (1964): 182-207; more broadly, Paul H. Meyer, "The Attitude of the Enlightenment towards the Jew," *Studies on Voltaire and the Eighteenth Century* 25 (1963): 1161-1205.

11. François Voltaire, *Philosophical Dictionary* ed. W. Baskin (New York, 1961): 5 308-309.

12. Isaac de Pinto, *Apologie pour la Nation Juive* (Paris, 1762) p. 28.

13. See Max Wiener, "John Toland and Judaism," *Hebrew Union College Annual* 16 (1941): 215-42; Alexander Altmann, "William Wollaston (1659-1724): English Deist and Rabbinic Scholar," *Jewish Historical Society of England Transactions* 16 (1952): 185-211.

14. See Arnold Ages, *French Enlightenment and Rabbinic Tradition* (Frankfurt am Main: Analecta Romanica 26, 1970).

15. Voltaire, *loc. cit.*

16. François Voltaire, *Letters of Certain Jews to Monsieur de Voltaire* (Dublin, 1777) 1: 62-63.

17. Christian Wilhelm Dohm, *Ueber die Bürgerliche Verbesserung der Juden* (Berlin and Stettin, 1781), pp. 143-44.

18. Zalkind Hourwitz, *Apologie des Juifs* (Paris, 1789), p. 38.

19. On Mendelssohn, see the magisterial volume by Alexander Altmann, *Moses Mendelssohn: A Biographical Study* (University, Ala., 1973); also M.A. Meyer, *The Origins of the Modern Jew* (Detroit, 1967) pp. 11-56.

20. Lazarus Bendavid, *Etwas zur Charackteristick der Juden* (Leipzig, 1793).

21. For example in [I.B. Bing], *Lettre du sieur I.B.B. Juif de Metz, à l'auteur anonyme d'un écrit intitulé: "Le cri du citoyen contre les Juifs"* (Metz, 1787), p. 7.

22. Zalkind Hourwitz, *Apologie*, p. 82.

23. *Pétition des Juifs établis en France, addressée à l'Assemblée Nationale, le 28 janvier 1790* (Paris, 1790), pp. 73-74. Although this petition may have been written for the Jews by their lawyer, Jacques Godard, it must have reflected the sentiments of the Jewish deputies and their general syndic who signed it.